Traditions of Caring

A HISTORY OF *Norse Home* · SEATTLE, WASHINGTON

Junius Rochester

Norse **F**

a retirement co

TOMMIE PRESS

805 32nd Avenue

Seattle, Washington 98122

Copyright © 2012

First Printing 2012

Printed in Canada

ISBN 978-0-9648950-7-2

Rosemaling cover artwork by Bernetta Pritchard

Table of Contents

Dedication

Thanks to **ELIE GLAAMEN** (1908–2010) for financing this historical project.

Elie was an example of the NORSE HOME history, as she grew up in Bleie Ullensvang Hardanger, Norway, and came to the Ballard area of the Pacific Northwest. She, like many other immigrants, wrote letters home about her experiences here and kept ties with her family in Norway. She was a talented seamstress and knitter and contributed many hand-made treasures to the Norna Ladies Auxiliary. Elie volunteered for and later moved to the NORSE HOME as a widow. At age 100, Elie taught herself how to use a computer and email while living at NORSE HOME. People remember her as warm, generous, kind-hearted and always ready for a good time! Elie was 102 when she passed away peacefully at the NORSE HOME. Her gift will help carry the NORSE HOME message forward.

Introduction

A Message from KONRAD URI, PRESIDENT, NORSE HOME BOARD OF DIRECTORS

This book is dedicated to all the men and women who cared so much about their friends and relatives in the Norwegian and surrounding community that they were determined to build a modern retirement home for them. This is also a rich history of Norwegians as immigrants, their sense of care and tradition of caring for their elders and their communities, and all they brought to the Pacific Northwest, including the NORSE HOME.

We gratefully remember the original core group of founders, who had all those meetings with interesting details to make a plan for this Home. We remember how they took on the task of raising funds to finance the building. It was a long process that started in the middle of the Great Depression of the 1930s and was completed in 1957.

We remember all who worked hard to keep the project going during the World War II years. With these historical pages, we also give thanks to those men and women who worked hard and believed in this project but did not live enough years to see its completion. I am certain that they would all be overjoyed to see that the mission they started was completed. It was the friends and family members of these individuals who then worked hard in the many early Guilds that persevered to see the building finished. These groups of women took charge of all the hosting of fundraising activities with their delectable Scandinavian hospitality, coffee and cookies for all.

This hospitality continues, and today the NORSE HOME lives up to its mission of quality affordable housing for all and is seen as a star among communities. The fact that the NORSE HOME is still recognized as one of the best places to retire and live has been the ongoing effort of the Board of Directors from the very beginning, as you will read in this history. The Board has worked hard to ensure that the people in charge of managing and caring for its property and residents do so with an understanding of its rich and special history.

We trust in our staff and volunteers to continue NORSE HOME's commitments. NORSE HOME creates loyalty among staff (those working for 20-plus and 30-plus years), the volunteers and the residents. There have been generations of persons from the same family living at the NORSE HOME. Sometimes I am asked, What makes NORSE HOME so special? It is hard to answer in just one phrase, but perhaps after reading our history and visiting the NORSE HOME for yourself (either in person or on our website), you will have that same understanding.

Proceeds from the sale of this book will benefit the RESIDENT ASSISTANCE FUND.

Prologue

This historical perspective tells the story of how the Norwegian traditions of caring not only for each other but for the elderly, evolved from a dream to a reality. There would be no NORSE HOME if not for the traditions of those before us and their beliefs in caring. It is necessary to begin the story of the NORSE HOME with a historical background of the Norwegian Mindset, their emigration to America, and their attraction to the Pacific Northwest.

To tell this story, our fictional hosts are two young Norwegians named HARALD LARSSEN and ANNA SAGSTAD. Harald was a native of Haugesund, a herring, fishing, and farming town on a sleepy sound; Anna came from a larger community, the busy port of Stavanger. Stavanger was a ship-building and canning center (today its economy is dependent upon the North Sea oil boom.)

In the late 1800s family members and neighbors were experiencing economic and personal hardships on family farms and in local communities. A desire for better conditions created an "America Fever" throughout Norway and other Scandinavian countries. In the New World there were new opportunities for food, survival and work.

We can imagine Anna and Harald were among those who left for America, at separate times, each on their own path. They had witnessed the upheaval and displacement among people around them. Through their fictional letters (typical immigrant stories), we learn about how they settled in the Pacific Northwest because of its familiar surroundings of water and mountains. They express their dreams and experiences (based on a combination of true life stories) in a series of letters in the beginning of each chapter.

You will read about key persons and organizations taking NORSE HOME from concept to completion. You will also learn the history of how it took several decades, many volunteers, countless hours of development and fundraising, and the names of important people behind each step.

The mission of NORSE HOME founders to create and have an affordable, non-profit senior housing community has been fulfilled since its opening in 1957. You will learn about the current day to day practice of the traditions of care and caring for the residents. This story shows the parallel progression of our fictional characters, ANNA and HARALD, from being immigrants, to being part of the Northwest community, to caring about the needs for a retirement home, and eventually becoming residents.

There are other real life stories at the NORSE HOME similar to our fictional characters. This remarkable history since its opening day, and until now, demonstrates the humble service to the community by an interactive staff enabling residents to live longer and happier lives.

Chapter I. The Norwegian Mindset

"I shall pass thru this way but once. Any good, therefore, that I can do, or any kindness that I can show to any human being, let me not defer or neglect it, for I shall not pass this way again"

— Anonymous

Anna's First Letter

Dear Uncle Per,

I still wonder why you chose to leave Vik for an unknown place so far away. My parents told me that many people in Vik have already boarded ships. Did you know some of those travelers? What did they tell you? My family is having difficulties and I am doing what I can to help, but more and more the stories of America are told in Stavanger. Our town, as you know, is a large port, so we hear from ship's crew and passengers about other places. I'm told that your town of Vik is having difficulty raising cattle and growing grain. Maybe these problems have caused you to look overseas. Please don't forget us and write home about what you see and do in America.

Anna

Harald's First Letter

Hello, Thorvald

The farms are so small near our town, and so many families need more room, that I keep hearing about people going far, far away where there is free land. Although herring fishing is good, my brother Nils is unhappy and has been talking to someone about leaving our family. Because America is so far away, I wonder if we will ever see him again. Today in school we learned about Viking trips to North America. Our teacher said that these voyages were also a result of poor land, perhaps too many families, and the search for places to catch fish. Will you visit me soon? We can talk about America and the Vikings.

Please write soon,

Harald

Immigrants
Is Everyone Descended From A Viking?

Seattle's NORSE HOME literature includes the self-descriptive statement: "A Retirement Community." Those three words are also on welcome signs at the NORSE HOME main entry.

Communities are built by people founded on shared history, interests and needs. The following story arises from the travels and hard work of countless Norwegian immigrants who came from the Old Country to the New World. Many of those individuals gave up most of their personal possessions to make this transition. Their story is the most recent in a long line of sacrifice and adventure, Old World to New.

Everyone claims roots. The more dramatic those family roots, the better the story. Seattle's NORSE HOME, founded by first, second, and third generation Norwegians (but open to all), proudly displays its Scandinavian roots. Casual discussions and organized activities at NORSE HOME often relate to Nordic roots that many residents share. Because everyone came from somewhere, and NORSE HOME residents have not forgotten their Viking past, it's worth taking a brief look at the legendary Norsemen and Norsewomen who moved about the (mostly) Western World.

The Viking period, AD 790s to 1060s, gave rise to many New World traits and customs. History makes that connection. And sagas, runic graffiti, artistic traces and, in a later period, letters to and from the New World, tell us the story of these extraordinary travel adventures.

EVERYBODY IS A VIKING

Seattle architect John Mahlum, son of Edward K. Mahlum, who designed NORSE HOME, said in a 2012 interview: "Everybody in Norway is related to a Viking." (He then opened his family genealogical notebook, which listed names stretching back to, believe it or not, Norse gods.) Similarly, among the many lessons ANNA and HARALD learned in school were the geography and history of their seafaring, farming nation.

THE NORDIC SETTING

Because of lingering northern glaciers, Scandinavia was buried under ice long after southern areas had produced busy human communities. Northern European lands were (and are) rocky, mountainous, bounded by wild seas, and not uniformly conducive to growing crops, grazing cattle or developing family-oriented settlements. Human survival was often the principal local activity. Young men from these brittle regions wanted land, mates and a better life. The harsh climate caused them to be hardy souls, ready for anything, fearing nothing.

Incursions southward — the first Nordic immigrants — by these restless gangs of men began in the early Middle Ages (about 600 A.D.). Many of these tribes roamed the waterways, either settling peacefully with local populations, or grabbing what they wanted through brute force.

After the fall of the Roman Empire (500 A.D.), Europe experienced a rise in temperature. The warmer climate suddenly produced perfect conditions for raising crops, including grapes. As sea levels rose, floods occurred in the Low Countries (e.g., Netherlands), causing settlements, including forts guarding against Viking raiders, to melt away — an open invitation to Viking visitors.

SAGAS, SONGS AND RUNIC CARVINGS

And why do many Seattle residents claim Viking heritage? The term itself may have originated within Scandinavia from *viking*, a pirate, or from the verb *vikja*, an inlet or bay. The Vik is a brawny bay leading to today's Oslo, Norway.

Bringing the story more or less up to date, until the 1840s, westerners had never heard of Vikings (centuries before, those who were invaded by the restless Northerners certainly knew them). Tales of Vikings reached European and American readers in the late 17th century. In fact, a famous book, *Chronicle of the Kings of Norway*, which was brimming with violent, wild stories, found a devoted public. When this reading craze quieted down, translations of sagas (stories told by elders during long dreary northern winters) and archaeological discoveries showcased a different Viking world. The revised picture was vivid, full of poetic and historical references, enhanced by images of natural sites. Here was also clear evidence of settlements, family life, arts and crafts, and sophisticated sea-going vessels.

Vikings left evidence of their talents as shipbuilders, mariners and designers. They also produced skilled craftsmen, artisans and woodcarvers. Viking women wore superior cloth garments and adorned themselves with imaginative gold and silver jewelry. A Viking cart found in the hold of a miraculously preserved ship held beautifully decorated sleighs with finely carved runners, animal head posts, artistically arranged geometric designs. Modern versions of those designs are reflected today in décor and celebrations at NORSE HOME.

Runic carvings added to these mysteries. Examples of runic graffiti, occasionally manufactured by jokesters, have been found throughout the Northern Hemisphere, even a short distance from NORSE HOME: a 1926 "discovery" near Spokane, Washington, of "Norse inscriptions" has been dismissed as a local prank.

THE VIKING PRESENCE

Of course, an introduction to NORSE HOME and its Scandinavian roots must include "Vinland," the name given to a likely landing on or near the North American continent by Leif Erikson. The name Vinland surely represents an area where grape growing occurred. Several legends related to that "discovery" suggest the native population was not pleased to see these strange, bearded giants in wooden boats. In fact, one version describes an Indian attack on the intruders, resulting in Viking deaths and injuries.

Among the most exciting and well-preserved Viking sites is *Anse aux Meadows* in north Newfoundland. Constructed about the year 1000 A.D., this temporary camp may have supported about 90 men, with a boat harbor, smithy, and kiln. What did this colony of rugged pioneers do here? No doubt they fished for cod; constructed and repaired boats; organized community meals (beginning a sense of community); held meetings, many of which were around rude maps; entertained each other with stories (sagas); and conducted musical and religious ceremonies. And despite their rough-and-ready bachelor existence, they practiced medicine and cared for ill neighbors — a precursor to NORSE HOME traditions.

Scholarship and science continue to find answers to the exciting Viking story. That's the pleasure and adventure of reading and listening. And NORSE HOME residents find these tales and much more in the house libraries. Many of those volumes are in the Norwegian language. And musical events, speakers, and celebrations — some of them 100% Nordic — add to the Scandinavian mystique and flavor of NORSE HOME.

LEIF ERIKSON

Leif Erikson, like Christopher Columbus, is an important name in the American story. Leif's saga is also associated with NORSE HOME and other Norwegian organizations. Defenders of Leif Erikson's "discovery" of America are legion. And that discovery may be true. Perhaps he was the first person to use the term "Vinland"?

Several historians point out that Erikson was probably seeking timber. Stands of useable timber in Norway were stunted and of little use in building boats. In fact, the importation of timber from North America to Norway — the main ship-building center in Scandinavia — had been underway for many years.

In about A.D. 1000 Leif Erikson may have sighted the North American continent, via Greenland. He also recorded seeing salmon, large lakes, vines and grapes in the "new" country. Call it luck or timing, Leif missed an encounter with what he and others called *Skraellings*, or local Indians. His brother,

Thorvald, following Leif's course westward, was not so fortunate. After a bloody battle, Thorvald was killed by a *Skraelling* arrow, the first recorded death in battle of a Viking in the New World.

Statues of Leif Erikson are found in American and Scandinavian locations. The Leif image known best to residents of NORSE HOME is located at Shilshole Marina. That sixteen-foot imposing figure, sculpted by August Werner in 1962, gazes over the North Pacific fishing fleet as they travel westward toward the majestic Olympic Mountains. The original base for Werner's statue was designed by Ed Mahlum, NORSE HOME's architect.

MYTH-MAKERS

In Old Norse, "Norway" (also known as *Novegr* or *Noregr*) probably meant the sea-lane, or the north way, along Norway's coastline. That sea-lane was an early path for Viking/Norwegian ship building and story-telling. As shipbuilding skills improved, and Viking knowledge of coastal waters grew, the first Norsemen ventured in many directions: south, east and, for our NORSE HOME story, westward. They not only brought utilitarian and artistic skills, but they also carried wild, exciting tales.

Among Norse myths was the belief that ravens — ubiquitous as blackbirds along the American west coast — would point the way to land. Those large ink-black birds were carried aboard ship, then released and followed to landfalls. In fact, the image of a raven often adorned Viking sails and boats and still decorates modern vessels.

Westward voyages were shrouded in myth, danger, violence and the unexpected. Viking images are part of North American history. With translation of the sagas in the 1840s – 1850s, myth-making grew exponentially. Many of those images blend into the story of Norwegian immigration to America, to Puget Sound, to NORSE HOME.

ANNA AND HARALD'S HISTORY LESSONS AND LETTERS

Norwegian schools teach their students Viking and North Sea history. An endless tale, the shipbuilding and sailing histories of Norway were familiar to every boy and girl. ANNA SAGSTAD and HARALD LARSSEN had been raised from birth with stories of oversea adventure and faraway heroes.

Before the 1800s, a rise in prices, shortages of grain, and the consequent decrease of foreign trade reminded Norwegians of the trials of their Viking ancestors. Most of the affected people in the 1800s were workers, fishermen, farmers and loggers. As conditions deteriorated, few of them had resources upon which to survive. A sharp and severe gap between wealthy and poor citizens caused restlessness, unhappiness, and occasional rebellion. ANNA and HARALD witnessed these conditions and occurrences.

Norwegian historian Odd S. Lovoll writes:

> *"The Viking past has in fact served as an effective symbol in Norwegian-American history... cultivation of the Viking image among Norwegian Americans is, however, more interesting in a different connection, for it reveals more about patterns of adjustment and efforts at self-assertion in an immigrant population than it does about actual historical parallels a thousand years apart."*

The eventual result of this modern day restlessness was the transfer of Norwegian people and culture, almost intact, to a New World. Our guides, ANNA and HARALD, found themselves in the midst of great changes. They described these changes in a trove of letters they wrote from America to loved ones in Norway.

Norwegians on the Move
From One Continent to Another

THE FIRST VISITORS TO AMERICA

The boats began to fill. In the 1840s, a Norwegian newspaper named *Christianssandsposten* began a series of stories about the New World. Letters continued to arrive from across the water, providing both information and entertainment to residents of Norwegian villages and towns. This activity was in line with a history of Norwegian visits to North America. Although the Dutch dominated the seas during the previous two centuries, Dutch ships often included Norwegian crews and officers.

After sporadic, and perhaps partially legendary, Viking incursions, Norwegians and Danes in the 1630s–1660s mingled with Dutch seafarers — who at the time were masters of the seas — to help establish the City of New York (once known as New Netherland and New Amsterdam).

FARMS AND OCEANS

John Mahlum wrote in a history he prepared about his father, Ed Mahlum, NORSE HOME architect: "Despite Norway's renown as a seafaring people since the Viking era, ninety percent of Norwegians were farmers in 1600. Farms defined ownership of Norway's land base, and in turn formed the basis for naming its people." Mahlum gives naming examples within his own family: Mahlum, Haave, Harvold, and Sondeled all come from a farm.

Two problems: 1) Many written records were lost or destroyed after Norway lost its independence to Denmark in 1537; and 2) Primogeniture — an exclusive right of inheritance belonging to the eldest son — caused younger siblings to look elsewhere for work and their future. One result of primogeniture was the emigration of sons (and daughters) to the New World.

ARRIVAL OF "SLOOPERS"

Later, the New World of the 17th century offered unusual opportunities to Norwegians and other Scandinavians to find a better life. Most historians put a date on that dramatic change: As noted before, October 9, 1825, was when the sloop *Restauration*, from Stavanger, Norway, dropped anchor in New York Harbor.

ANNA and HARALD had studied the Sloopers in school and learned more about them in America. This famous event consisted of fifty-three passengers and crew. The little 39-ton ship's fourteen-week voyage brought an extra passenger: A child was born in the mid-Atlantic. Many of the passengers were Norwegian Quakers (Society of Friends) seeking religious freedom. Their story was familiar to the pages of history. Religious oppression, escape, and relocation were as American as apple pie. America had long offered a haven for political and religious dissenters, renegades, social outcasts, and the best and truest farmers and city-dwellers aspiring to a better life.

The "better life" sought by Sloopers first had to run a gauntlet of local misunderstanding and government paperwork. Local authorities complained that the ship was "overloaded," imposing a fine of $400. After the Sloopers petitioned President John Quincy Adams, the fine was suspended. That gutsy request to the President sent a signal that the Sloopers were quickly learning how to make their way in the New Land.

Slooper reenactments have been held many times, including in ANNA's home town of Stavanger, Norway, (with King Olav V, Crown Princess Sonja and Crown Prince Harald participating on July 4, 1975). Other local reenactments occurred in Silvana and Poulsbo, Washington, USA, to help celebrate the 1975 Norwegian Immigration Sesquicentennial, known as N/A 150.

Like Norwegians in later years, many of them later moved to America's Middle West. As new arrivals relocated from place to place, aboard ships or across dry land, they looked after one another in the same spirit demonstrated at today's NORSE HOME. Caring for one's neighbor, as one would a family member, was Norwegian custom.

A LARGER PICTURE

Looking more closely at the Norwegian story — because the 1800s witnessed a great migration from all Europe to the United States — there were signs of discontent and upheaval. Norway, far to the north of its neighbors, had long been a successful trading partner with the rest of Europe. In the early 1800s, however, she lost her neutrality after inadvertently becoming involved in her neighbor's wars.

Economic growth stagnated, prices of goods abruptly rose, and many Norwegians faced a bleak future. The Danish-Norwegian union, with Denmark the senior partner, was causing strains between the two countries due to the centralization of economic and cultural affairs.

On May 17, 1814, Norway separated from Denmark. The two countries participated in a constitutional assembly convened at Eidsvoll, Norway. Hence, Norwegian Constitution Day is celebrated on May 17 (*Syttende Mai*), a landmark day enthusiastically observed at NORSE HOME and with a parade in Seattle's nearby Ballard community since 1889.   The new constitution was modeled after notable documents, several of them from the American continent:

1. The Constitution of Massachusetts, 1780;
2. Montesquieu's Principles of Separation of Powers, 1748;
3. The U.S. Bill of Rights and U.S. Declaration of Independence, 1776;
4. The French Proclamation of Human Rights, 1789.

The May 17 milestone was celebrated in a song written by Nordahl Grieg, Norwegian World War II hero:

> *"Bare today is the flagstaff*
> *Where Eidsvoll's trees show green,*
> *But never as now have we fathomed*
> *What the blessings of freedom mean.*
> *A song through the land is swelling,*
> *Of victory's hour it spoke,*
> *Though only by closed lips whispered*
> *Under the Foreign yoke."*

VISIONS OF AMERICA

With the European population explosion between 1750 and 1850, a new strain was put on economic uncertainty in Norway and elsewhere in Europe. The Industrial Revolution, at top speed in England, began to leave less developed countries behind. (In the late 1940s, five years of foreign occupation also put a strain on the Norwegian people.)

The United States offered distressed Norway and other European nations an attractive option with its progressive, open society. The result is a matter of record: Between 1815 and 1915, thirty-five million emigrants came to America. Many NORSE HOME residents and their families hold memories of this dramatic period through oral traditions, scrapbooks and old photos.

The new adventure was also advertised via letters to the homeland. Letters sent with loving, informal, detailed descriptions of a new life and unlimited opportunities became popular reading throughout Norway. Like an erratic telegraph message, many letters were copied and sent from town to farm to church. One Norwegian 17th century immigrant writer put it this way: "Any poor person who will work diligently can become a well-to-do man here in a short time." ANNA SAGSTAD and HARALD LARSSEN participated in this written discourse.

Besides the letter campaigns, and mostly good news from America, there were homegrown problems contributing to emigration. For example, Norwegian population growth exceeded resources and job opportunities, and impoverished citizens were having difficulty rising above their station. Although Norwegian authorities were unhappy with the exodus, no serious official steps were taken to stem the flow.

Crossing the Atlantic Ocean was often an ordeal. For example, it was a daunting experience to face two months sailing, with illness, sea sickness, occasional deaths and births, poor food, and unsanitary conditions. In the mid-1860s, steamships began to replace sailing ships. This innovation increased the emigration tide. At first, most emigrants sailed from Gothenburg, Sweden, or Le Havre, France, to the province of Quebec, Canada. From there, hardy travelers made their way to the United States. After the Civil War period (late 1860s), most Norwegian immigrants sailed directly to New York City.

SPIRITUAL INFLUENCES

The Lutheran Church's role was important and lasting in the Norwegian immigrant story, as it has been in the establishment of the NORSE HOME.

The first glimmer of Scandinavian organized religion in America occurred around 1657, when a petition was presented to the Dutch colonial government asking for the services of a Dutch Lutheran minister. Struggling to overcome resistance from the Dutch Reformed Church — originally a State Church — Lutherans eventually emerged as a spiritual presence in the colonies.

Odd S. Lovoll and Kenneth O. Bjork, writing for The Norwegian-American Historical Association in 1975, claimed that "A unique immigrant culture evolved [in America], elements of old-country heritage mingling subtly with American influences. Out of a Lutheran state-church tradition emerged a free church, split into a number of synods with conflicting theological positions... [this evolvement], combined with the necessity of newcomers to adjust to the American environment, resulted in the founding of numerous academies and colleges."

Historians have also pointed out problems with a "free church," which many younger immigrants found exhilarating. Author Jon Gjerde writes: "It might be argued that the church schisms in fact allowed for the creation of synods and congregations that were perhaps more responsive to parishioners' needs. Members of church congregations, moreover, were allowed to oppose their clergy if they felt they were in error." That "freedom" was a long stretch from strict aspects of certain Lutheran churches in Finland and other countries, which in some cases held that blasphemy — i.e., swearing — was a punishable sin.

ALL FAITHS

Roman Catholicism, Judaism, Society of Friends (Quakers) and other faiths found the Norwegian homeland — and later the New World — favorable environments for growth. Of course, Catholics today have strong ties to Norway and America.

Nils E. Boch-Hoell, writing in a 1980 edition of *The Norseman*, asserts that World War II (1940–1945), with Norway occupied by German forces, had an effect on religion. He states that "The Church of Norway was informally organized as an anti-occupation front under the leadership of a 'Common Christian Council.'" He quotes a letter of protest issued by the bishops of Norway that included the following: "When the authority of a society permits violence and injustice and God's commandment is set aside and sin appears, the [Lutheran] Church, which is the custodian of conscience, can never be silent." The result was that copies of this letter were confiscated by German police, and bishops and pastors were refused admittance to their churches or exiled from their dioceses and parishes. In April 1942, most bishops resigned, followed by 93 percent of the clergy.

TAKING CARE OF EACH OTHER

Like their Viking ancestors, Norwegian emigrants looked after each other aboard ship and in their temporary New World communities. Visitors suddenly appearing on American shores were sometimes resented and looked at with suspicion by the native-born. Newcomers often did not speak English, cherished Old World folk medicines, and had a background of personally caring for family members and neighbors. Eventually, immigrants founded health, social and cultural organizations for their particular national groups.

In Seattle, and over several decades, these organizations included individual lodges of the Sons and Daughters of Norway, The Sons of Norway, The Daughters of Norway, The Norwegian Hospital Association, and NORSE HOME.

Another form of assistance was Death Benefit societies to help indigent families pay for a proper burial and provide funds to destitute families following the death of a family member. Such societies were formed by Norwegians (and others) to ensure that the family of a deceased person would not fall into poverty. These services and benefits emerged from larger immigrant associations in an effort to help members survive family emergencies and local economic hard times.

THE *BYGDELAG*

Seattle also was the scene of a *bygdelag*, a society formed to host family and Old Country reunions and to perpetuate aspects of Norwegian heritage.

On August 1, 1920, a small group from Oppdal, Norway, met for a Sunday picnic and *bygdelag* in Woodland Park, Seattle. A constitution was adopted, officers elected, and a publishing program launched. The coincidence of this early meeting in Woodland Park, later the neighborhood of NORSE HOME, was not accidental. Woodland Park, across the street from NORSE HOME, has long been a meeting and recreational center for Norwegian and other immigrant groups. It continues in those roles, with the addition of providing a stunning territorial view for NORSE HOME residents who look out the building's east windows.

It's true that early Norwegian emigrants sought "Old Country" jobs in the seafaring, fishing, timber, and farming professions. But soon they — and certainly their children — quickly adapted to all American economic rhythms and opportunities.

With education, which was universally encouraged from the home, later generations entered every field. Norwegians (and other Scandinavians) emerged in American politics, business, military, mining, medical and legal professions, cultural affairs (such as music and fine arts), and education, to cite only a few examples. Accomplished and influential men and women who helped build NORSE HOME are cited in this story.

TWO-COUNTRY LOYALTY

Patriotism became a byword, while Norwegian immigrants simultaneously cherished the virtues of a rich heritage and looked to the *bygdelag* as a touchstone with Norwegian traditions.

In 1917, just before America's entry into the Great War, Norwegian organizations publicly affirmed their loyalty to the new country. Traditional festivities and celebrations were sometimes canceled, because, as one immigrant spokesman wrote, "we don't want to give anyone opportunity for misunderstanding, but prove that we are citizens of this country." Official support was given to the Red Cross, while campaigns to buy Liberty Bonds and War Savings Stamps were highlighted. During World War II, 1941–1945, the successful campaign to raise money for NORSE HOME was put on hold, while attention was given to home defense efforts.

During a 2012 interview for this book, Trygve Kvalheim, Norwegian immigrant, master carpenter, and former NORSE HOME Board president, asserted that once he had chosen to live in America, his loyalty was to his new home. Despite his cultural and family ties to Norway, Kvalheim said that America came first.

Despite struggling to survive, learn, protect their families, and achieve recognition from neighbors and employers, native Norwegians and subsequent generations looked after kin and neighbors. That tradition — caring for the elderly, orphans, people with illness, and retirees — remains firmly in place today. NORSE HOME is only a recent, specialized example of care and caring by Norwegian families.

BETWEEN TWO COUNTRIES

ANNA SAGSTAD and HARALD LARSSEN, like all immigrants, were caught between two countries and two cultures. Their separate westward journeys created challenges and caused the two young people to make new choices every day. They had in common a devotion to the Lutheran faith. In Norway both had worshiped with their families in local churches. As they moved through the newness of America, they frequently stopped at local Lutheran churches, halls, or church-sponsored civic organizations. Of course, ANNA and HARALD also shared a growing bilingual life, ANNA catching on to English colloquialisms faster than HARALD, perhaps because of the years she spent in a bustling, international port town. The "immigration" experience began to permeate their lives, first as outsiders, then as part of a growing floodtide of wide-eyed North American residents settling into routines of school, marriage and patterns of work. Disappointment and confusion occasionally interfered with their progress, but help was always nearby.

Chapter II. Looking for Common Ground

"And now that I'm used to the climate,
I think that if man ever found
A spot to live easy and happy,
That Eden is our Puget Sound."

"I laugh at the world and its shams,
As I think of my happy condition,
Surrounded by acres of clams."

(Excerpted stanzas from "The Old Settler" by Francis Henry, 1860s.
This poem was adopted by restaurateur Ivar Haglund as his theme
song; the last three words were used to name his restaurants. Inheritor
of a Norwegian background, Ivar served as Honorary Campaign
Chairman at the NORSE HOME's 25th Anniversary Dinner — and
belatedly celebrated his own birthday — on June 5, 1982.)

Harald's Second Letter

Hello, Thorvald,

You asked me to tell you about my life. That is difficult because nothing
stays the same in America. God be praised, I am in good health and enjoying
meeting new people every day. I found boat work in Poulsbo, Washington
but it was not my dream job. While looking for other chances I visited
Seattle across the water several times. This big city looks like Oslo.
It has everything with people going back and forth in trolleys that rattle
and shake. One town near Seattle is called Ballard. Many Norwegians
live there and most of them work at shingle mills or in the boat-building
and fishing industries. The mills have many jobs but I might prefer to
build boats. You know that my wood working skills were learned as a boy
in Haugesund. Next to downtown Ballard is a long waterway that may soon
connect the city's large freshwater lake to salty Puget Sound. I found
a room of my own next to Ballard's Vasa Hall, where on several evenings
I listen to a Norwegian band play. At the Hall, I met a girl named Anna
from Stavanger. She is learning to become a nurse. Love to everyone and
tell my brother I made it to America.

Harald

Anna's Second Letter

Dear Momma and Papa,

Several girlfriends asked me to join them in learning more about our new big city. We took a train called the Interurban from Seattle to the small town of Fremont. It was a slow ride, surrounded by hills and lakes. We saw people fishing off docks. Several of them seemed to be local Indians with dark skin. After leaving the Interurban we climbed aboard a private trolley that took us up a hill to a large park. The park and its woods are on the top of the hill. This beautiful place also has a zoo. Later we walked into the town of Ballard following a group we met in the park to a hall where we listened to Norwegian music. Ballard is like Stavanger. Almost everyone speaks Norwegian and there are restaurants serving food from home. At the dance hall a man played tunes I recognized. Several couples danced but I talked to a tall man named Harald. He told me about crossing Puget Sound in small boats and that he lived in the town of Poulsbo which reminded him of a Norwegian town.

Last week I started studying to be a nurse with the help of two Norwegian women at a Seattle hospital called Sisters of Providence. Most of the hospital staff is Roman Catholic. The last three Sundays I attended Immanuel Lutheran Church near the small lake where I saw men fishing. The church services are conducted in Norwegian. Please tell Uncle Per that I'm reading English language headlines.

Anna

Puget Sound Vibrations
A Reflection of Scandinavia

PETER PUGET'S WORLD

Why Puget Sound? The first stops of Norwegian immigrants other than Quebec and New York City were often the open country, towns and cities of America's Midwest. A number of forces affecting Norwegians were in play during the mid-1800s. Europe's economic, military and government upheavals and problems took a toll on the average citizen. France, Germany, Great Britain, the Netherlands and Italy reached across the globe in a rush to colonize and dominate weaker countries. Industrialization was under way, creating social, cultural and civic unrest.

In contrast, the American open frontier looked exciting. During the 1840s and 1850s the Oregon Trail beckoned. The 1850 Oregon Donation Land Law invited pioneers to the Oregon Country (today's Oregon, Washington and parts of Idaho, Montana and Wyoming) on favorable terms. Later, the Homestead Act of 1862 promised free land. By the 1860s the railroads were blatantly and enthusiastically advertising the wonderful American West. Because most immigrants were farmers, the attraction of fertile soil was an effective sales pitch.

Like almost every other ambitious person in the U.S., when gold fever hit California, Idaho, Oregon, Montana, British Columbia, and Alaska, Nordics streamed to these areas. Some hardy men, and a few women, overtaken by the gold bug, decamped to Northern California (Sacramento) around 1849, moved to the Pacific Northwest in the 1860s, Frazier River, Canada, in the 1870s, and then boarded boats for Alaska (Klondike, Skagway, Nome) in the late 1890s. San Francisco and Alaska inherited Norwegian traditions and small settlements as a result of this race for riches. Odd S. Lovoll, in *The Promise of America*, names Norwegian Jafet Lindeberg (mistakenly called Swedish in several accounts) and two Swedes, Erik Lindblom and John Brynteson, as the discoverers of gold on the Seward Peninsula (Nome). They staked claims on and near Anvil Creek for themselves and for others using a Power of Attorney.

MID-WESTERN FLAVORS

ANNA SAGSTAD was excited to arrive in America and find a job in North Dakota. She was one of many Norwegians who seized opportunities offered in the American frontier. The Midwest — i.e., Illinois, Wisconsin, Minnesota, the Dakotas, Nebraska and eastern Montana — beckoned to early Norwegian immigrants. Besides the attraction of open agricultural land, Norwegians emerged in large cities in search of manufacturing and industrial opportunities. Several of these centers would become famous for their immigrant neighborhoods and organizations: Chicago, Philadelphia (where *Societas Scandinavensis* was established in 1769), Boston (the site of an early Norwegian society in 1853), Minneapolis, San Francisco, and, of course, Seattle.

Early immigrants also tried their luck in the Mississippi and Missouri river valleys — the so-called Homestead Act Triangle. Winters were severe. Those who chose to live in a sod house, as ANNA did, on a treeless, windswept prairie, often struggling with land that had been burned out from intense cultivation, sometimes lost heart. Later arrivals in the Dakotas and elsewhere began to scan the horizon. The view westward appeared inviting because of the mountains and water.

In 1910, 80 percent of Norwegian Americans (from a total of about one million) lived in the Midwest. By the 1980s, the Norwegian American "capital" was Minneapolis. Those hard-working souls were the "New Vikings." Most of those adventurers emigrated from Norwegian rural areas and distant upper reaches of fjords, yet many of them quickly adapted to American urban life.

THE FAR CORNER OF AMERICA

Besides the "letter campaign," so-called Norwegian "pathfinders" roamed the open country, describing wonders of the New World, especially Puget Sound and its verdant surroundings. Pacific Northwest fjords, tree-laden hills, snowy mountains, islands, navigable bays and inlets struck familiar chords with Norwegian immigrants. A Snohomish County, Washington pioneer wrote: "The jagged summits of the Olympics now appeared clear and cold, sticking out of the dark, green bank of firs on the foothills. I thought of Norway." Puget Sound, besides being a Horn of Plenty, had the right "look."

By 1910, Norwegian language newspapers were available in the Pacific Northwest. These papers printed subscribers' letters about Puget Sound — part of a relentless letter-writing campaign. The Brooklyn newspaper *Nordisk Tidende* (Nordic Times) was among the first to appear. In Pacific Coast regions, *California-Posten* (1876) led the way, followed by Seattle's *Washington-Posten* (1889) and *Tacoma-Tidende* (1890). Seattleites also read *Western Viking*, billed as "the oldest Norwegian newspaper in America," and *Scandinavian American*, under the heading "Serving the Scandinavian-American Population of the Great Northwest." Besides keeping in touch with the Old Country, these publications swung from liberal to conservative in their politics, depending upon the arrival of a new publisher or editor, but they relentlessly and frequently featured letters written by immigrants.

Several letter writers were rhapsodic about the Pacific Northwest's idyllic climate, and boasted how easy it was to become "assimilated and Americanized" in the Far Corner. A few brave scribes were not shy about favorably comparing Washington state with the Dakotas and California (citing occasional water shortages in the latter). In a "Letter from the World's End" (Lake Ozette, Olympic Peninsula), Severin Jerstad cited a nearby English school and a Norwegian Lutheran association as attractions for Norwegians.

THE PALOUSE

Wheat farming was a familiar Norwegian occupation. The rich wheat country of the Palouse (eastern Washington state) drew many immigrants. Those lands, now largely farmed by corporate interests, support a thick layer of loess, or wind-blown soil. Production of wheat can reach 80 bushels an acre in good years (100 bushels in the valleys). Individual Norwegian farmers moved to the Palouse, as did small utopian communities of immigrants.

POULSBO

Founded by Norwegian immigrant Jorgen Eliason in the 1880s, Poulsbo, Washington, has retained its Nordic themes in architecture, celebrations (e.g., the Annual Viking Fest), and culinary delights. Norwegian immigrants found the nearby bay and hills a perfect Nordic fit. Agricultural and fishing opportunities also attracted them to this pristine area.

In 1891, Lutheran pastor Ingebrigt Tollefson founded a Lutheran orphanage in scenic Poulsbo.

Less than twenty years later Ebenezer Rest Home was constructed on the same site and incorporated as an "old folks' home." The corporation received support from churches throughout the Puget Sound area and the Midwest. In the mid-1940s, the Martha-Mary children's orphanage was closed, while Martha and Mary nursing home continues today. The facility is run by a corporation, the West Coast Lutheran School and Charity Association. The Board of Directors comprises delegates from nine Lutheran church congregations, all in Kitsap County. General features of Martha and Mary were incorporated into NORSE HOME, especially the tradition of caring for elder citizens.

King Olav V, as part of a national tour, visited Poulsbo's Grieg Hall for a public luncheon on October 20, 1975, to help celebrate the Norwegian American Anniversary or Sesquicentennial, called N/A 150 (1825-1975). On other occasions he and members of his family toured NORSE HOME.

TACOMA

Norwegian colors have long flown in Tacoma, Puget Sound's city with the deepest harbor (Commencement Bay). Fishing, boat building, general construction and farming attracted immigrants to this city. At one time, Tacoma was Puget Sound's busiest municipality. Valhalla Temple, Tacoma, Washington, hosted the founding of *Nordfjordlaget* in 1915 (*lag*: a society or societies comprising members from a specific Norwegian region). Longtime officers included many who would later play leading roles in founding and operating Seattle's NORSE HOME.

NORWAY HALL, SEATTLE

Built in 1915, Norway Hall stands today in the center of Seattle at 2015 Boren Avenue. It once housed the cultural and fraternal societies Leif Erikson lodge of Sons of Norway and Valkyrien Lodge of Daughters of Norway. Designed by a Norwegian, E. Sonnichsen, the structure is a "medieval type of house still to be found in Norway."

Norway Hall is considered a "loft," built to perform dual functions: storerooms and living and sleeping quarters. The Hall tends to follow a Norwegian romantic revival tradition incorporating elements of a "dragon" style seen in early stave churches. Decorative elements included carved dragons (now gone) and sawn balustrades. Once a busy center of Norwegian immigrant dances, celebrations and ceremonies, the Hall has passed through several owners. A Landmark Nomination Form notes that Norway Hall "is a monument by and to the Norwegian[s]… dedicated to their devotion for [a] new homeland, and to their contributions to the enrichment of our city."

In 1925, a group of about thirty Norwegian immigrants met in the Hall and signed up for a *Sondmorslage* (now called *Summorslaget*). Those founders were former residents of Sondmor, Norway, who wanted to preserve their Old World customs and stay in touch with each other. Another activity — helping each other in case of sickness, loss of a job, or family death — was similar to the foundation and origins of NORSE HOME. Picnics were sponsored by the group, attracting people from Tacoma, Olympia, Grays Harbor and Everett, Washington.

BELLINGHAM

The Stavanger *Lag* of the West Coast was organized at Bellingham, Washington, on February 15, 1917. One convention is held each year. This *Lag*, or cultural organization, preserves the Norwegian language and culture and adheres to a spiritual path. (ANNA SAGSTAD arrived too late to participate in her hometown *Lag*.)

STANWOOD, CAMANO, SILVANA, NORMA, CEDAR HOME AND THE SKYKOMISH AND STILLAGUAMISH DELTA

Norwegians found good soil, water access, and pleasant surroundings in what was referred to as "The Delta." The nearby Stillaguamish River was locally referred to as the "Stilly." Many of these neighbors were old friends and often related to one another.

Sivert Brekhus and his son John, after a stop in Chicago, established a home on the Stilly. They cut trees in every direction to establish their farm. Oxen and donkey engines dragged logs and stumps into a "rig pile" for burning.

Ole Fjarlie, a Stanwood pioneer, lived over 100 years. He was the first president of *Vestkystens Nordmorslag*. The organization had its first meeting at Vasa Hall in Ballard on January 12, 1936. U.S. Senator Henry M. "Scoop" Jackson was a member, as was his mother, Marine Andersen. Silvana's Viking Hall was the site of many Old Country entertainments. The Stanwood Historical Society continues to help preserve the town's pioneer immigrant roots.

People Coming Together

Organizations Are Formed

NORWEGIAN COMMERCIAL CLUB

Founded by a group of men in the Masonic Order under the name Odinian Society (named for the Nordic god Odin), the Norwegian Commercial Club held its first meeting on November 16, 1932. In the Great Depression, Norwegian business people in Seattle realized that improved commercial success might be realized through cooperation. The Club originally consisted of "men of Norwegian birth and ancestry." Over the years Club officers participated in the founding and operation of NORSE HOME, including Trygve Jorgensen, later Board President at NORSE HOME.

Spreading its wings since its founding, the Norwegian Commercial Club today lists its "Objects and Purposes" as:

> *"To promote and encourage civic and commercial activity to the end that benefits therefrom may accrue to the State of Washington, City of Seattle and the Pacific Northwest."*

The Club has not drifted far from its Norwegian roots, noting that it intends to maintain a social and business club "for Norwegians, Norwegian-Americans and others."

SANGERFESTS; THE NORWEGIAN MALE CHORUS OF SEATTLE AND THE NORWEGIAN LADIES CHORUS OF SEATTLE

Organized on December 6, 1889, The Norwegian Male Chorus is the oldest a cappella male chorus in Seattle. The founding date, Dr. Alf Knudsen pointed out, was "six months after the founding of the City of Seattle and three weeks after the State of Washington was admitted to the Union." Knudsen also pointed out that singing in the Norwegian Male Chorus "can be addictive." As an example, he cites Harry Solheim, a member for over 80 years, and his father, Gustav Solheim, both of whom sang with the organization. The Male Chorus has participated in almost every local *Sangerfest* since its founding. On January 19, 1975, the Chorus appeared at Norway Center for the opening ceremony of the National Norwegian-American Sesquicentennial. That same year it participated in a program re-dedicating the statue of Edvard Grieg on the University of Washington campus. The Chorus often practices and performs at NORSE HOME, using the large dining hall with its resonant acoustics. The "Singers' Helpmates," a ladies auxiliary of singers, was organized in 1909.

August Werner, founder and longtime director of The Norwegian Ladies Chorus, wrote: "It isn't often in our lives that an idea is carried out with complete success… It isn't often that a project, with no ulterior motive, no scheme for material gain — it isn't often that such a project bears fruit." Norwegians are traditional music makers, and the Ladies Chorus has made itself available to every possible Nordic event since its founding in 1936.

DAUGHTERS OF NORWAY

Beginning in 1905, the first Daughters of Norway of the Pacific Coast lodge was organized in Seattle. In 1907 it took the name Valkyrien Lodge No. 1. (*Valkyrie*: maidens of the Nordic god Odin who conducted slain heroes to Valhalla, hall of the dead). Two more Daughters lodges were organized, chartered by the Sons of Norway of the Pacific Coast: Embla Lodge No. 21 in Tacoma, and Freya Lodge No. 3 in Spokane. On February 20, 1908, the three lodges incorporated as Daughters of Norway on the Pacific Coast. Its mission: hold annual conventions; promote social and cultural exchanges among its members; maintain a fraternal burial fund.

In December of 1908, Valkyrien Lodge paid $1,000 toward purchase of property on Boren Avenue, Seattle, for the construction of Norway Hall (opened in 1915 — noted earlier). The cost was shared equally with Leif Erikson Lodge No. 1, Sons of Norway of the Pacific Coast. The mortgage was paid off on January 12, 1921.

Five western states eventually participated. The individual lodges: Valkyrien, Seattle, Washington (1905); Embla, Tacoma, Washington (1907); Stjernen, Astoria, Oregon (1910); Breidablik, Seattle, Washington (1910); Gjoa, Oakland, California (1913); Solheim, Butte, Montana (1913); Camilla Collette, Silvana, Washington (1923); Thelma, Everett, Washington (1908 – Affiliated 1931); Crown Princess Martha, San Leandro, California (1956); Sonja Henie, Sparks, Nevada, 1971.

The purpose of the lodges expanded to promote the aims of the Order and to take part in community affairs. For example, in times of national emergencies members have given financial aid and service to both their native and adoptive countries and have sponsored a scholarship program for advanced studies. These same purposes were applied to the founding and operation of NORSE HOME.

Illustrating the Daughters' deep commitment to Norwegian culture, it wasn't until 1936, at the Daughters' 20th Convention at Seattle's Olympic Hotel, that it was agreed to translate the organization's Constitution and Ritual books into English.

Important dates of the Daughters: April 7, 1951, Norway Center at 300 Third Avenue West, Seattle, was dedicated by Leif Erikson Lodge and Valkyrien Lodge; December 10, 1955, participated in the NORSE HOME groundbreaking and is listed as a founding member of NORSE HOME; September 2011, Valkyrien moved its belongings and functions from the Nordic Heritage Museum to NORSE HOME.

SONS OF NORWAY

The Sons of Norway began as a Grand Lodge in Minneapolis, Minnesota, in 1895. As the Norse population grew in the Far West, interest in establishing a local lodge grew.

The first Puget Sound effort was *Den Norske Forening* in Everett, Washington, which was turned down by the Minneapolis group. At first, bylaws of the Sons of Norway required members to purchase life insurance policies issued by the Grand Lodge, and perhaps it was believed that the far-away Pacific Coast was an unlikely place to sell these instruments.

After that rebuff, an independent organization was established called Grand Lodge, Pacific Coast, followed by Leif Erikson Lodge No. 1 in Seattle. A.A. Anderson was elected the first president of Leif Erikson and the inaugural meeting was held at Forester's Hall, 818 First Avenue, Seattle, on May 13, 1903.

Kristine Leander, in *Images of Seattle*, writes that "Clubs such as the Sons of Norway actually started as mutual aid groups for Norwegians with wage loss, sickness, or death." An example cited earlier: Death Benefit Societies.

The second Pacific Northwest lodge was Norden Lodge No. 2, Tacoma (1904). The western groups, after several years of growth and maturity, took the position that the life insurance program should be voluntary, an argument they eventually won.

An important role of Leif Erikson Lodge No. 1 would be to serve as a principal founder of NORSE HOME.

NORWAY PARK

In 1952, members of the Leif Erikison Lodge No. 1 helped found Norway Park, north of Arlington, Washington. This was once the site of a logging operation on Lake McMurray. John Olsen, resident of NORSE HOME and a former NORSE HOME Board Member, is a shareholder in the Norway Park Corporation. John wrote and recorded a brief history of this area. He tells the story of oxen pulling wagons loaded with timber to nearby sawmills. The early loggers, John states, were Norwegians, Finns and Poles. Today the community is an active recreational center for Norwegian-Americans and their guests.

ALASKA-YUKON-PACIFIC EXPOSITION

Norwegians came by the thousands to participate in and enjoy Seattle's AYPE in 1909. Cheap railroad fares encouraged Norwegians from across the nation to visit the Pacific Northwest during the Exposition. August 30 was Norway Day at the AYPE. On that occasion, a historically accurate reproduction of a 60-foot Viking ship, built at Ballard Boat Works by Sivert Sagstad and manned by forty modern-day Vikings, sailed into view "majestically around the bay off Laurelhurst." On the same afternoon, the St. Olaf College Band entertained guests, followed by an evening performance of the United Norwegian Singers of the Pacific Coast before 20,000 guests in the Natural Amphitheatre (site of today's Padelford Hall). The Expo recorded 42,026 visitors on Norway Day. On the same day, Norwegian folk costumes were displayed in windows of the downtown Bon Marché department store.

NORDIC HERITAGE MUSEUM

Webster Elementary School saw hundreds of Norwegian children in its classrooms for many years. When the school closed its doors, the sturdy building reopened as the Nordic Heritage Museum in 1980. Again, a Scandinavian organization was developed by a group of visionaries meeting over a cup of coffee. Besides being a supporter of NORSE HOME, the Museum takes pride in displaying, preserving and celebrating the heritage of Norwegians, Swedes, Danes, Finns, and Icelanders. Each of these nations has displays of their own within the building. The Museum's library is distinguished by a variety of titles related to the Norse experience. Classes in rosemaling (decorative designs from Norwegian rural areas), cooking (both Scandinavian and Viking), knitting, woodcarving, and Nordic languages are taught each week.

NORSE HOME and Museum events also offer opportunities to sample original foods such as lutefisk, dried Norwegian cod soaked in a lye solution. This famous dish is often served with lefse, a thin bread made from rolled dough. Other favorites: herring, salmon, cod, halibut, cold ham, lamb, and beef. Cheeses are favorites, especially goat cheese (*geitost*). Cranberries are a staple. At adult gatherings, a touch of *akevitt* or beer is welcome.

CHURCHES

Following are a few examples of local churches supported by Norwegian immigrants and their families. These spiritual groups in no way make up a complete list of religious figures and organizations that have supported NORSE HOME over many years.

An overview: In 1900, there were seven Lutheran Churches in Seattle. By 1910, eleven more had been established. Added to this mix were Methodists and Baptists who had Scandinavian missionary activities on the West Coast. The new America and its challenges tended to release many immigrants from their traditional religious ties. For example, in the early 1900s, secularization had increased, resulting in about 15 percent of Norwegians in Washington state claiming membership in a Lutheran congregation.

One of the earliest Seattle churches was Denny Park Lutheran, founded as the Norwegian-Danish Evangelical Church in 1888. Denny Park was Seattle's first public park and the site of its first cemetery (since moved), given to the city by pioneer David T. Denny.

Immanuel Lutheran Church opened in 1890. It stands today near the south end of Lake Union in the Cascade neighborhood. This proud institution became the home of the Reverend Hans Andrew Stub from St. Paul, Minnesota. After greeting his eleven parishioners in 1901, Stub went to work. He reached out to younger people, gave sermons in both Norwegian and English, and extended assistance to the underprivileged. No one was turned away. Immanuel Lutheran, under the Rev. Stub's direction, eventually saw standing room only crowds on Sundays. He also played an active role in helping establish NORSE HOME and its traditions of caring. The Reverend Stub and his wife later lived at NORSE HOME, where he occasionally conducted Vesper services and served as counselor to fellow residents.

Founded in 1894, Ballard-First Lutheran grew from a merger between Zion Norwegian Congregation (1894) and Bethlehem Norwegian Congregation (1906). Ballard-First Lutheran, at 20th Avenue Northwest and Northwest 65th Street, has close ties to NORSE HOME.

Although it's not a church in the accepted sense, the Rev. Olai Haavik started a religious celebration in 1929 that has grown and become an integral part of the Norwegian community — the Blessing of the Fleet at Fishermen's Terminal, Shilshole Bay.

FAMILIAR AND COMFORTING SOUNDS

Among the sounds and influences appreciated by Norwegian immigrants was the voice of Oscar Marcos Jorgenson. Each week day in the 1940s, Jorgenson would ride the bus from his home on Queen Anne Hill and put in his hours as a clothes salesman at Seattle's well-known Lundquist Lilly store. After work he would walk a few blocks to the Skinner Building on Fifth Avenue. Having learned Norwegian and Swedish as a boy from his grandparents, he would enter a sound booth at 6:00 p.m. and report the day's events to an enthusiastic listening audience in the Old Country languages. He began his program with KXA, later switching to KJR. His comments were interspersed with phrases of traditional Nordic music, principally from the keys of an accordion, and with brief interviews (in Norwegian) of friends. Occasionally his family would join him in the studio, remembering to remain absolutely silent. The family would then walk to the area of Fourth Avenue and Pine Street for dinner.

Jorgenson's popular program was discontinued during World War II, when foreign languages were banned from American airwaves.

THE NORWEGIAN HOSPITAL ASSOCIATION

A sign of care and concern for the elderly and others can be seen in The Norwegian Hospital Association (also described in the chapter on Women/Guilds). Its purpose was to raise funds for the establishment of a non-sectarian hospital in Seattle. Six Norwegian women met on January 7, 1913, and incorporated an organization a few months later. In December 1922, the hospital building was purchased at 3515 Woodland Park Avenue North in Seattle.

Looking at the historical background, it's likely that the women who founded Seattle's Norwegian Hospital Association and the small Norwegian Hospital knew of similar projects in the Midwest. For example, Chicago was the site of the Norwegian-American Hospital, which opened its doors in 1895 as the Norwegian Lutheran Tabitha Hospital. In the 1920s, clinics and hospitals were opened by Norwegian immigrants in Madison, La Crosse and Eau Claire, Wisconsin. These traditions and policies were later incorporated into activities and purposes of NORSE HOME.

ANNA AND HARALD SEE THE FUTURE

ANNA considered her fate in America. Because of her youth, she didn't give much thought to health issues or old age. Finding work and the daily excitement of the New World filled her hours. In time, she learned how her Norwegian brothers and sisters, especially women, organized professional groups to take care of the sick and elderly. Likewise, HARALD rarely considered these matters, until the day came when he needed professional help at reasonable cost. Many years down the road, both ANNA and HARALD would find the care and concern they needed at NORSE HOME. And they kept their families informed about these matters in letters they wrote to the Old Country.

Seattle: The Queen City

City; Town; Neighborhood

UPHEAVAL

HARALD and ANNA's travels revealed interesting lessons about how the Pacific Northwest of America's corner emerged from a violent geological past.

The Pacific Plate has been nudging under the North American Plate for eons. Volcanic turmoil preceded and followed this relentless activity. Earthquakes — and Seattle has its share — are reminders that several faults are buried beneath our beautiful world, including a deep east-west line through the waist of Seattle called the Seattle Fault.

An ancient geological show was provided by the Vashon Glacier, which advanced and receded, leaving mountains, lakes, rivers, landslides, a beautiful sound, and a rock-strewn backyard similar to Norway. When Vashon began to melt about 14,000 years ago, gravel, silt, and water everywhere became Seattle's natural inheritance. As the Vashon Glacier melted past the San Juan Islands, the sea (Pacific) filled in behind it. We call that body of water Puget Sound, named for Captain George Vancouver's trusted officer, Lieutenant Peter Puget. When one is gazing westward at this shimmering pond through NORSE HOME windows, it's hard to believe the violent details about its birth.

NATIVE RIGHTS

ANNA STAGSTAD watched Indian fishermen on the shores of Lake Union. There are dramatic stories told about the Natives' 13,000-year existence in the Pacific Northwest. For example, Indian neighbors tell about vanishing islands, tsunamis, tidal waves, and heaps of shoreline debris resulting from ancient violence. Seattle's first residents, called the Duwamish and Suquamish, began to arrive here from Asia. They have been around long enough to witness unusual natural occurrences and to pass stories along to young ears.

A glance at the aboriginal world — and a few pioneers saw it — included forested shoreline, fish and game everywhere, and stands of Douglas fir, hemlock, cedar, maple, ash, and oak. Wildlife included deer, bear, coyotes, raccoons (still with us), mink, otter, and birds galore. The Audubon Society suggests that Steller's jay, blue heron, quail, eagles, humming-birds, swans, and tule wrens had the run of the forest and pathways.

THE OUTSIDERS

And then strange visitors arrived. Norwegian and other immigrants would follow these early explorers. In the 1700s, Spanish, French, English, and Russian ships sailed by what would later be called the Washington state coast. The first Euro-Americans to "discover" Elliott Bay and Seattle probably were John Holgate, Luther Collins, Henry Van Asselt and Samuel Mapel in the 1850s. Claims were established first in the Duwamish Valley, followed by Alki Point and the Seattle waterfront. At this point we learn the names of William N. Bell, Carson D. Boren, and Arthur and David Denny.

From most sources, it appears Indian and white residents got along. In fact, old Chief Seattle became a pal of David S. "Doc" Maynard. Maynard talked the chief into using his name for the new settlement. The native name had been "Dewamps" (people living on the river), later pronounced "Duwamish" by the newcomers. Commerce took off when Henry Yesler arrived and built his sawmills. Both native and white employees found jobs at Yesler's mills.

The gates were now open to pioneer settlement. The timing was right for Norwegian and other immigrants to find land and a new life along the shores of Puget Sound.

NORDICS ON THE SCENE

Perhaps Capt. George Vancouver had a couple of Norwegian crewmen aboard when he sailed the Strait of Juan de Fuca (1792). The same might have been the case aboard the U.S. Exploring Expedition (1841), skippered by Lt. Charles Wilkes. Beyond speculating about those two famous mariners (both of whom named Puget Sound landmarks), it's virtually impossible to provide details about the first Norwegian settlers in the Queen City area. For instance, single Norwegian men no doubt visited the Puget Sound area in the 1850s seeking adventure or the Main Chance.

Norwegian visitors began to leave a record of their arrival on Pacific Northwest shores. The volume *Vikings and their Descendants* lists Martin Toftezen, who settled in "Washington Territory… around 1850," a date that matches the timing of Seattle claims by founders John Holgate, "Doc" Maynard, and the Denny party. Norwegian Knud Olson and his brother-in-law purchased a home from Catherine and David "Doc" Maynard at 3045 64th Avenue SW, Alki Point, in 1868. (The Olson home is considered Seattle's oldest building.) Olson's real estate deal occurred soon after the Dennys and others staked claims abutting Seattle's muddy tidelands.

The name of Norwegian immigrant Henry Peterson emerges in this early period. He and his wife, Mary (Thompson) Peterson, apparently met in Seattle around 1875 and later resided at 14th Avenue and Madison Street. Henry and his brother Lewis became well-known photographers. Several of their photos are in the Museum of History and Industry (MOHAI) collections.

James J. Hill's Great Northern Railroad reached Seattle in 1893. This was an important milestone, because Norwegians would soon come aboard the new St. Paul-Seattle link, including ANNA SAGSTAD and HARALD LARSSEN.

HARALD arrived just before Ballard was annexed to Seattle in 1907. However, he saw and later worked near the large C.D. Stimson cedar shake mill at Salmon Bay, Ballard. So did many other Norwegians with strong backs and deep experience in wood working, boat building and fishing. The Stimson mill would become the largest of its kind in the world, and jump-start Ballard's prosperity. By the early 1890s, a third of the nation's cedar shingles came from Ballard. Most of Stimson's employees were Nordics, and most of those workers had Norwegian backgrounds.

Coincidentally, the national financial Panic of 1893 also occurred in the inaugural year of Hill's Great Northern, which gave rise to an unusual story: Robert E. Ficken and Charles P. LeWarne, in *Washington: A Centennial History*, describe the incident as follows: "Shingles were accepted by merchants in lieu of cash and in church collection boxes."

Following the Seattle Fire of June 6, 1889, many Scandinavians came to Seattle for promised high wages in rebuilding the city. Unskilled laborers earned $2.00 to $2.30 a day; skilled workers $4.00 to $6.00 a day. Compared with the national average weekly earnings of $8.88 (1892), Seattle became a magnet to newcomers. After the Panic of 1893 had subsided, the Alaska-Yukon Gold Rush in 1897 pulled Seattle out of its economic doldrums with interest. The arrival of Scandinavian seamen after 1900 substantially added to those who came by rail or around Cape Horn (South America) by ship.

SCANDINAVIANS WORKING TOGETHER

In the 1870s, volunteer women formed an experimental organization called the Emigration Society. It operated as an informal board of immigration, helping Seattle newcomers of all backgrounds find employment, housing and medical care — a precursor to a role later played by NORSE HOME. Following the lead of this organization, in 1876 a Scandinavian Immigration and Aid Society was founded by Andrew Chilberg, who later became the first Swedish-Norwegian consul in Seattle. Mentioned previously, Norwegian newspapers in Seattle and Tacoma provided useful information — in the Norwegian language — and acted as civic boosters of the Puget Sound region.

Some of the following events and individuals have been mentioned, but the early 1900s — when HARALD LARSSEN and ANNA SAGSTAD were learning about Puget Sound country — witnessed a number of Norwegian milestones: Leif Erikson Lodge of the Sons of Norway was established (1903); the first Pacific Coast Norwegian Singers Association Sangerfest was held in Everett (1903); The 1909 AYPE featured Norwegian culture and a "Viking" ship; Daughters of Norway met for the first time in 1908; Scandinavian Studies were introduced to the University of Washington curriculum in 1909; in 1910, it was estimated that Scandinavians were the largest ethnic group in Washington; Norway Hall opened for business in 1915; and Mayor Ole Hanson was elected in 1918, just in time to become immersed in the Seattle General Strike and the rhetoric of journalist Anna Marie Strong, who participated in what was called a national "Red Scare."

BALLARD

NORSE HOME, sitting atop Phinney Ridge, boasts a spectacular view westward over the Ballard neighborhood, formerly an independent town, with Elliott Bay and the jagged Olympic Range in the background. Known as Seattle's historic Scandinavian center, Ballard hosts Norwegian Constitution Day celebrations with a Market Street parade on May 17. The Nordic Heritage Museum is nearby.

During the 1860s, shareholders formed a subscription library as a counterweight to the raucous, bachelor neighborhood. On June 4, 1904, a new Carnegie Library opened, featuring a "Men's Smoking Room" and a "Ladies' Conversation Room." Trolleys ran north to the outskirts of town (near the present location of NORSE HOME and Woodland Park) and south to the burgeoning metropolis of Queen City Seattle. This busy, independent scene changed when Ballard was annexed by Seattle in 1907.

Ballard's Salmon Bay waterfront, home of the C.D. Stimson and other mills, was a lively neighborhood by the late 1890s (and remains today a center of trendy restaurants, bars and clubs). In the early years, retail shops, livery stables, bordellos, and saloons lined nearby streets, most of them serving employees of the shingle mills. Ballard was known to old-timers as "Snoose Junction," because smokers were not allowed near the tinder-box mills and piles of cedar shingles at Salmon Bay. In 1895, a local paper described the Shilshole scene:

> *"The air is filled with the dissonant music of the 'panting' of the steam jets,*
> *the buzz of the circular saw, the singing of the knee-bolters, the grinding of the chains."*

BRIDGES AND LOCKS

On November 10, 1911, a momentous local event occurred with the opening of Hiram M. Chittenden locks. Fresh and salt water briefly mixed as Lake Washington and Lake Union dropped nine feet. Now a water path was cleared, allowing ships to move in four directions on two lakes through linking channels. Private waterfront properties and city-owned parks and recreation areas began to burst with activity. HARALD had noted the likelihood of this nautical route in one of his letters.

The Ballard Bridge opened in December 1912. The bridge's bascule lift spans and counterweights firmly established a land link between north and central Seattle. Railroading, another transportation activity, attracted Norwegian engineer Andreas Wendelbo Munster in 1906, followed by Norwegian surveyor Martinus Stixrud.

Seattle's Fremont Bridge opened on June 15, 1917. Spanning the Lake Washington Ship Canal, this bascule bridge (counterbalanced with weights, like a seesaw) was originally painted blue and orange. The colors were selected by Fremont residents in a poll. It remains one of the busiest bascule bridges in the world — opening and closing about 35 times a day. With the opening of the Ballard and Fremont Bridges, Seattle's North End, especially Nordic neighborhoods, were quickly integrated into the larger city.

MEMORABLE PERSONALITIES

Martinus Stixrud designed railroad switchbacks, platted Seattle's Denny-Blaine Lake Park subdivision, surveyed Seattle's waterfront, and developed a plan to widen the Duwamish River. (A curious story associated with Stixrud: He died of a brain hemorrhage in 1901 at age 47. His remains were allegedly sent back to Norway, but a tombstone bearing his name can be seen today in Seattle's Lake View Cemetery on Capitol Hill.)

Although many Norwegian Ballard residents worked in sawmilling, fishing, crabbing, and other maritime industries, many Ballard citizens branched out in different fields.

One such individual, and a longtime supporter of NORSE HOME, was Ole Bardahl. After settling in Ballard in 1922 as a Norwegian immigrant without knowing a word of English, and building a successful construction business, he bought a chemical company that produced soap and an oil additive, the latter product becoming popular with owners of motor cars. Bardahl eventually oversaw worldwide distributorships of his handiworks. He (and his products) gained wide fame when he entered boats in Unlimited Racing in 1957. Ole's first Miss Bardahl won a national championship. His other boats were also successful, especially as participants in the Seattle Seafair celebrations. Upon Ole's retirement in 1969, he had won more unlimited powerboat races than anyone else in history.

FISHING AND SHIPBUILDING

Halibut fishing was dominated by Norwegians. It was estimated by fishing expert A.K. Larssen that "around 1920, 95 percent of all halibut fishermen and an even higher percentage of local boat owners were of Norwegian birth or descent." Springtime saw the fleet, after being blessed by a local pastor, sailing from Fisherman's Wharf Dock, near Ballard, for the season in Alaska.

Shipbuilding in Ballard became famous. The high reputation of this profession attracted HARALD LARSSEN. His hardy companions spun tales, knew their way around the world, and were pleased to teach young HARALD the secrets of wood-working tools and boat design. Several boat works (which still occupy space in Salmon Bay) achieved a reputation for seaworthiness and utilitarian styles throughout the world.

To illustrate the range of boats launched in Ballard, the following details describe three famous vessels that sailed from Salmon Bay and achieved wide attention:

1. The so-called *Viking Ship* was constructed by Sivert Sagstad at Ballard Boat Works for the 1909 Alaska-Yukon-Pacific Exposition. The ship arrived with a great deal of anticipation and to the cheers of several thousand Norwegians and others as she approached the Exposition grounds by water.

2. Rear Admiral Richard E. Byrd used the Ballard-built *USMS North Star* on his 1939-1941 Antarctic exploration. The 1,434-ton wooden ice ship was originally built in 1932 for the Bureau of Indian Affairs, U.S. Department of Interior, to run summer supply routes in Alaska. After the Byrd expedition, the *North Star* stopped at the Panama Canal, New Zealand, Pitcairn Island, Easter Island, and ports on the Chilean coast before returning to Seattle. She returned to duty in Alaska in 1941.

3. In 1911, a fishing vessel named *FN Tordenskjold* was launched in Ballard. Today (2012), it is one of the few survivors of many such working boats sent to distant ports. The *Tordenskjold*, according to Pacific Fishing magazine (April 2011), "leads a small fleet of

hard-working commercial fishing schooners that compete head to head with modern boats on the Alaska fishing grounds." This rugged, seaworthy vessel is celebrating her centennial and showing no signs of slowing down. The *Tordenskjold* was likely the handiwork of our letter writer HARALD LARSSEN and his co-workers.

MEDICAL CARE

When ANNA SAGSTAD entered nurses training in Seattle, she contended with a global mix of nostrums, personal habits, and rudimentary science. Norwegian and other immigrants arrived in the new country seeking a better life, but they shared basic needs: jobs, food, shelter, education. Without bodily health, the other factors could break down. Kay Nelson, in *Passport to Ballard: The Centennial Story*, outlined the mix of Old World remedies and American medicines and treatment for a host of medical problems.

Nelson cites mustard, bran and oatmeal for poultices; salt for hot packs and gargles; cayenne pepper and egg yolks and whites were cure-alls for other troubles. Norwegians arrived with packets of healing herbs, such as mandrake root, dandelion, burdock, chamomile, sassafras, red clover, and rhubarb. One of the most interesting practices was applying the fur side of a muskrat skin against a person's cheek to mitigate asthma attacks.

Opium and morphine were available as anesthetics, and sometimes abused for personal use. Nelson writes that "dope fiends" were often put on trolleys by the police with "enough fare to get away," which, of course, was not a long-term resolution of the problem.

Quarantining contagious patients meant stay-at-homes had to be kept from town. If the contagious disease was serious, Ballard had devised a floating "Pest Island" in Salmon Bay (which at one time broke its moorings and floated into Elliott Bay with frightened patients aboard). Small local medical facilities appeared: Ballard Private Hospital in the early 1920s, Lebanon Home (started in 1908 at 1500 Kilbourne Street, but operating in Crown Hill until 1938), and Firlands Sanitarium, opened in 1911 in North Seattle.

Although Ballard struggled to protect the health of its citizens, the Great Depression caused dislocation and personal loss. Instead of cash, doctors were paid in merchandise, including pickles, halibut, salmon, cookies and chickens. With the opening of Ballard General Hospital, medical help became more professional and available.

Dr. J. Hans Lehmann, in his charming autobiography, *Time Out of Joint*, describes details of his fledgling medical practice on Ballard Avenue. Dr. Lehmann wrote: "My wonderful Norwegian lumber mill workers and fishermen soon became the bulk of my growing practice and their trust and loyalty never ceased to inspire me." Dr. Lehmann would later play a key role in building the services and reputation of Ballard General Hospital, now a branch of Swedish Medical Center.

THE NORSE HOME NEIGHBORHOOD

"It is good manners which make the excellence of a neighborhood. No wise man will settle where they are lacking."

— Confucius, 500 B.C.

NORSE HOME windows provide four-way views of the Queen City. When the Phinney Avenue property was purchased by NORSE HOME representatives on January 23, 1938 (more detail follows), NORSE HOME founders took advantage of a convenient trolley line on Phinney Ridge next to Woodland Park, one of the city's spectacular greeneries. This fortunate choice of a site yielded views of Scandinavian Ballard, salt and fresh water courses surrounding Seattle, and two mountain ranges: the Olympics (west) and the Cascades (east).

Besides views of nature and the byways of a great city, NORSE HOME'S neighborhood holds a fascinating history of human activity. Woodland Park, which has been called "the best known, most cherished park and largest recreation grounds in the (Seattle Parks and Recreation) system; the pride of the citizens," has been host to an interesting collection of people and animals. Several individuals from this neighborhood — and a few notable wild animals — left their marks on Seattle history. The park also impresses ANNA, who with her friends walked the paths of this landmark, eventually trudging downhill to the busy town of Ballard.

GUY CARLETON PHINNEY (1852-1893)

Canadian immigrant Guy Phinney (from Nova Scotia) saw what other newcomers discovered in the pleasures and opportunities of Puget Sound country. He and his wife, Nellie, had no reservations about living in "the country." Seattle was nearby, but forested land and a sparkling lake to the north of the little town seemed like the perfect place to raise a family. Phinney purchased 188 acres in the late 1880s, which he called Woodland, later renamed Woodland Park.

Descriptions of Mr. Phinney describe him as "a man of vision and great energy." He was also described as weighing 275 pounds with a height of six-foot-three-inches. In 1880, Phinney built a wood sawmill on Lake Washington at the foot of today's Charles Street. After acquiring wealth he sought a baronial estate, allowing him to construct a great mansion, hunt wild game, introduce a "zoological park," and putter aboard his steam-operated launch on a body of water — shimmering Green Lake. After the Great Fire of 1889, he bought Woodland Park, which included a half-mile of frontage on Green Lake.

Loggers had taken the largest trees on Phinney's estate, leaving smaller ones as a private forest. Within one year, Phinney had invested $40,000 in his country estate. Before his project was complete, he decided to open his grounds to visitors. His next challenge was getting Seattleites to visit the park.

Other investors at this time made an important discovery: trolley cars. After 1889, electricity was proven successful in moving these rattling conveyances along tracks. In Seattle, the Second Avenue to Jackson to Leschi Park route was the first, followed by lines to Madison Park; to Madrona Park; from Seattle to the town of Fremont; followed by a web of additional routes.

The Seattle-Fremont trolley line ended, of course, in the thriving, quaint village of Fremont. Guy Phinnney laid his own trackage from the main gate of his estate at Fremont Avenue and 50th Street to the town of Fremont at which Phinney erected a granite archway with the date 1889 on the top — a few short blocks east of NORSE HOME (the archway was removed in 1912, one of many Park "improvements" over several decades). Fremont passengers from Seattle then boarded Phinney's trolley car and lumbered up the hill. Readers will recall that ANNA and her friends disembarked the Interurban in Fremont and boarded Phinney's little trolley for their visit to Woodland Park. Phinney's trolley was known in the neighborhood as the "White Elephant" and was operated by a motorman named W.W. Grass. Mr. Grass also took Mr. Phinney to his office in the Post Building at Yesler Way and Post Street (later destroyed in Seattle's Great Fire — the first new downtown building to rise after the fire was a two-story brick structure on First Avenue, erected by Phinney). When the Phinneys attended the theater downtown, their private trolley (and Mr. Grass) was standing by.

Although Phinney welcomed visitors to Woodland Park, guests were required to observe rules of behavior. Examples: Dogs would be shot on sight; no firearms; no picking flowers, cutting or marring trees, plants, benches or buildings; drinking fountains must be turned off after use; buggies were only allowed on designated roadways; molesting of animals was forbidden; profane or vulgar language was prohibited; no gambling.

Guy Carleton Phinney died unexpectedly in 1893, leaving his wife to cope with their sprawling estate. After doing her best, Nellie gave up and sold Woodland Park to the City of Seattle for $100,000. Woodland Park was the first major playfield, swim beach (Green Lake), and boating and fishing facility to come under Parks Department jurisdiction.

REINDEER AND SAAMI

The Woodland Park story includes several links to Norwegians: a meeting place for picnics and celebrations; the *bygdelag* held on August 1, 1920; the Park's proximity to Scandinavian Ballard; establishment of the 1913 Norwegian Hospital on nearby Woodland Avenue; and NORSE HOME across Phinney Avenue from the Park.

However, perhaps the most unusual Nordic story related to this large park concerns the March 7, 1898, arrival of 500 reindeer. Woodland Park was chosen as a grazing and rest stop for these exotic animals during their extraordinary journey from Norway to Alaska by ship and train.

Dr. Sheldon Jackson, a Presbyterian missionary and Alaska Superintendent of Education, observed during a visit to schools on the Arctic coast that Inupiat Eskimos were facing a food shortage due to the overhunting of whales, walrus, and caribou by commercial hunters. His solution was to import reindeer. His first specimens were obtained from the Chuckchee herders of eastern Siberia. The responsibility for introducing and caring for the reindeer was given to the Office of Education in the U.S. Department of Interior. After experimenting with small herds on Alaska islands, a total of 1,280 were brought to the Alaska mainland from Siberia.

Woodland Park, once Guy Phinney's pride and joy, had a relatively wild woodland and pasturage. In other words, it was just right for a herd of deer. Local newspapers described the unusual party, emphasizing the traditional colorful Saami garb worn by the herders. Crowds of people gathered in the Park to see this strange sight.

JOHN C. OLMSTED (1852-1920)

Norwegian and other Seattle leaders were looking forward to the 1909 Alaska-Yukon-Pacific Exposition. In preparation for the Grand Show, the Olmsted Brothers landscape architecture firm from Brookline, Massachusetts, was hired in 1902 to take a look at Seattle's parks.

John C. Olmsted, the lead designer dispatched to Seattle, was the stepson of Frederick Law Olmsted. The senior Olmsted, with Calvert Vaux, designed (among many sites) New York City's Central Park; Prospect Park in Brooklyn, NYC; South Park, Chicago; Morningside Park, New York. Frederick on his own designed Mount Royal Park in Montreal, Canada, and Tacoma Land Company, Tacoma. With his stepson, John, the elder Olmsted laid out the Stanford University campus, Palo Alto, California; the World's Columbian Exposition (1893), Chicago, Illinois; and the famous Biltmore Estate in Asheville, North Carolina.

Olmsted's "Comprehensive System of Parks and Parkways" was adopted by the Seattle City Council in 1903. In the case of Woodland Park, Olmsted's plan objected to trolley lines within the grounds. Instead, it suggested that "ridges and valleys be preserved as natural undergrowth and trees restored. The upper level of the park (nearest NORSE HOME) and lakeshore should be planted to lawn or grass. In the upper area should be provided a formal garden."

In 1922, Olmsted's recommendation about a "garden" was realized when the Seattle Rose Society suggested a Civic Rose Garden. That formal garden can be seen today, a short walk from NORSE HOME, a special summer treat for NORSE HOME residents.

Olmsted was also commissioned to prepare landscape plans for individual parks and playgrounds in Seattle. Thirty-seven such units were developed by the end of 1930. Woodland Park was one of them. Regarding the zoological garden, Olmsted suggested that only the Park's upper level be used for "a collection of hardy wild animals." And so it was.

THE BURNING FERRIS WHEEL

Before NORSE HOME and apartment houses were built along Phinney Avenue, the ridge boasted a bona fide amusement park. Several NORSE HOME residents have recalled what happened here or have heard the story. Occasionally the location of the Ferris wheel is confused with the present site of NORSE HOME.

Lucy and George Vincent had been operating a neighborhood carousel and Ferris wheel about one block north of NORSE HOME's current location since 1919 (at North 55th Street). Their entertainment center included, besides the famous Ferris wheel, a confectionary/lunch counter called the "Orange Thirst Shop" and a roller-skating rink. The Vincents' operation was called Woodland Park Pavilion or Woodland Amusement Park.

On the evening of August 26, 1934, the carousel and its pipe organ, the skating rink, and most spectacularly, the "Vincent Ferris Wheel" went up in flames. The Seattle Post-Intelligencer called it a "three-alarm fire." The sky lit up, attracting thousands of spectators from throughout the city. According to the P.I. story, "special police details were called on to hold back the throngs…" A weird and strange accompaniment to the conflagration was caused by "screaming animals" in the Woodland Park Zoo.

The Seattle Fire Department, despite the brief arrest of what they described as a 23-year-old "mental defective and confessed pyromaniac," listed the cause of the fire as "Unknown." The loss to the buildings and contents was $38,000. The amusement park never reopened.

ANIMALS IN THE ZOO

Noted above, residents, staff and visitors to NORSE HOME have always known about the nearby "wild kingdom." Whether or not they visit the park and zoo regularly, many are pleased to be on the hill next to one of Seattle's special natural outdoor attractions.

In passing, it's worth noting several famous early wild residents of the Zoo. A popular attraction was a pair of ostriches in what was called "Phinney's Zoo." These exotic, long-necked creatures enjoyed strutting before fascinated visitors. Among other animal stars was Tusko, billed in the 1920s as "The Biggest Elephant on Earth." Perhaps to counter that Big Guy, a "midget" elephant born in India, was purchased in 1920.

And many remember "Bobo," a more-or-less domesticated male gorilla purchased from a family in Anacortes. "Bobo" was often dressed in human garb, and during his young years attended birthday parties of human fans. Having been raised by humans, he cavorted shamelessly for peanuts and attention. In 1957, the year NORSE HOME opened its doors, "Bobo" became a local TV star. He can be seen today, stuffed and silent, in the Museum of History and Industry.

These neighborhood wonders were — and are — shared by NORSE HOME residents and staff. In fact, in the late 1980s a "Zoomobile" was used by residents to visit Woodland Park. A story in the December 1989 *NORSE HOME Retirement Center NEWS* states: "To our knowledge, no other retirement center in the entire world has an internationally recognized zoo right across the street. Where else can curious residents board an electric tour cart and be driven by a special attendant to see lions, apes, giraffes, elephants, and other exotic creatures in natural habits. It's like taking safari in less than a day."

KING OLAV V

On May 1-4, 1969, King Olav V of Norway visited Seattle and noted that it was a "friendly place." After the usual formal dinners and downtown ceremonies, punctuated with toasts and speeches, the King attended a gathering at the statue of Leif Erikson, Shilshole Bay. He then toured NORSE HOME on Phinney Ridge, enjoyed watching animals in the Woodland Park Zoo, and had lunch at the Space Needle.

At Norway Center, after listening to the Ballard High School Band and the Issaquah High School Chorus, the King complimented everyone by expressing appreciation for Seattle's success in preserving Norwegian traditions.

(King Olav V had visited Seattle previously as Crown Prince in 1939 and 1942. The 1942 visit was particularly poignant as German troops were occupying his country.)

FINDING THEIR WAY

ANNA SAGSTAD and HARALD LARSSEN watched Seattle and Ballard grow. They each had witnessed the great Ferris wheel fire on Phinney Ridge and the commotion surrounding that event. And they experienced separate and shared experiences among the flower beds and trees of Woodland Park. Their children became fans of the park's zoological gardens. Nearby Green Lake seemed like a diamond in the midst of busy streets and new homes. The lake was, in its early days, a favorite fresh water fishing site. HARALD knew how to anticipate the seasonal salmon runs in Elliott Bay. And the Norway-like climate, caused by the Olympic Mountains' "rain shadow," helped allay ANNA's and HARALDS's initial homesickness and worries about the families they left behind. In their letters to Norway, they told their families these stories, featuring Woodland Park, Ballard and the Nordic-like surroundings.

Chapter III. Call To Action

LA OSS SAMFUNNET TRYGGE ---

GI FULLT AV VAAR TROHET, VAAR EVNE OF AAND

(Let Our Society Be Safe…

Give the Full Strength of Our Faith, Our Ability of Spirit)

(From the Poem by Robert Ashton Moen,
Dedicated to the Supporters of NORSE HOME)

Anna's Third Letter

Dear Momma and Papa,

Harald and I will be married in two months at Immanuel Lutheran Church in Seattle. My only regret is that you and my Stavanger friends cannot attend the ceremony and party at Norway Hall. The other news is that Harald has learned to dance. We attend Norwegian celebrations at Norway Hall. Some of these gatherings are for fun and dancing. Others are held to discuss ways to assist new immigrants find work and medical care. One discussion I attended was about establishing a home for older Norwegian folks.

Harald has already built 12 wooden fishing boats which are used to go to Alaska and catch salmon and halibut. Most of the time the fish are processed in Alaska, but when there is enough fish he brings them back to share with our friends in Ballard. So many miles and years have passed since I left Norway, but America has given me a new life.

Anna

Harald's Third Letter

Hello, Thorvald

You will not believe it but in a few months I will marry a pretty girl from Stavanger. She is a nurse and will take care of me forever. Her name is Anna Sagstad and she has many friends. She also taught me to dance without stepping on her feet. Anna and I will live in a white house near the Government Locks.

Yesterday I helped launch a large fishing boat from my company's way in Ballard. I made it from bottom to top — as a ship under construction should be built. My boss, Ole, tells me this vessel is the finest fishing boat the company ever launched. Our business is good, but another company called Foss with strong Norwegian connections, is a major competitor.

Seattle has become a very busy place ever since a great fair was held on the new University of Washington campus years ago. Many people are moving here, including Norwegians from Wisconsin, Chicago, and New York. It seems that everyone has heard about Puget Sound because it looks like Norway. Please tell your parents about my new life and marriage.

Harald

The Task
NORSE HOME Awakening

A GOAL

Among many changes in Seattle that HARALD and ANNA witnessed were more efficient efforts to welcome and help Norwegian immigrants. Each of those efforts took time, but new Americans learned to be patient.

According to great philosophers, patience is a virtue. The Norwegian founders of NORSE HOME were endowed with unlimited patience, and were therefore probably deemed virtuous people. On the other hand, unexpected events can delay progress, thereby imposing patience on individuals. Perhaps it was a little of both circumstances that caused the dream of an "old folks home" for Norwegians in the Pacific Northwest to experience a 29-year gestation period.

To help trace steps leading to the founding of NORSE HOME, old documents, letters and minutes were read, complemented by "Old Timer" interviews. Many of the paper records were undated, but other written comments helped corroborate details and clarify the NORSE HOME path to success.

A SUMMARY

Initial discussions regarding founding a retirement home for elderly Norwegians began in 1928, just prior to the Great Depression. The project was finally realized after World War II and in the midst of the Korean War. The NORSE HOME dedication ceremony was held on June 15, 1957. Because of this stretch of time, the project occasionally seemed beyond reach.

In spite of America at war or busy with postwar rebuilding, and with Europe in turmoil marked by a periodic scarcity of funds, the determination of the Grand Lodge of the Order and Sons of Norway Lodge No. 1, later joined by many other individuals and organizations, never faltered. NORSE HOME was going to be built!

Why did the Sons of Norway and others advocate the NORSE HOME? Donald Thoreson, Seattle attorney and former NORSE HOME board member, explained why he supported the idea and the concept of care for elder citizens. First, he did legal work for NORSE HOME, which gave him a close look at the needs of seniors. Second, he recalls his mother and dad looking after their parents until they died. Thoreson was imbued with the immigrant and Norse tradition of caring for others, especially family members. Konrad Uri, Board President of NORSE HOME, remembers that a Norwegian tradition of lending a hand is time-tested. Offering such assistance included feeding neighbors (often with fish from the holds of vessels) and donating clothing.

ROOTS

The Sons of Norway, Leif Erikson Lodge No. 1, was formed on the Pacific Coast in 1903. Upon celebration of the Lodge's 25th anniversary in 1928, the idea for a retirement home was introduced. This concept was raised at the District 2 Convention of the Sons of Norway Lodges. An early typed history of that meeting outlines the idea of a "home for elderly Norwegians," which was "well received by the delegates, but because several members could not agree on the location of such a home — whether to build it in California, Oregon or Washington — the plan was (temporarily) abandoned."

On April 10, 1929, a Committee of three persons was selected to revive the question of an "old people's home." The Committee consisted of Kornelius Johnson, Ivor Thorson, and Abraham O. Kvalheim. Just over two weeks later, on April 24, the Committee chose May 8, 1929, as the next date to "take up this matter." Information cards with details about establishing a retirement home were sent to all members.

The Sons of Norway Lodge No. 1 held a special meeting on May 8, 1929, to discuss the retirement home idea and outline what the role of the Lodge might be in this endeavor. That meeting resulted in the following suggestions:

1. Unanimous approval was given to the idea of building a home;
2. The means to achieve this goal would be by private subscription (tabled);
3. The proposed home should be primarily for members of the Order, and that "entrance fees" would be charged residents;
4. It was proposed that Lodge No. 1 contribute $500 per year for ten years, but was changed to $1,000 per year for the same period.

SUBSTANTIAL LEAPS

In 1931, during a Sons of Norway "Boundary Picnic" at Lake Goodwin (ten miles north of Everett, Washington), the subject of a local home for retired Norwegians was again discussed. It was proposed that the location of such a home "should be in the Puget Sound area." Although a Committee had already been formed (April 10, 1929, above), leaders of attending groups reformed (or rededicated) an organization to pursue the retirement home idea. One early "history" states that Abraham Kvalheim was confirmed as the Committee's chair or president.

ABRAHAM O. KVALHEIM (1884-1957)

Born in Norway, Mr. Kvalheim came to the United States as a teenager, first settling in Maddock, North Dakota. He moved to Seattle, Washington, in 1925. During the founding years of NORSE HOME, Kvalheim was chairman of its first Organizing Committee. He served NORSE HOME as treasurer and longtime president (ten years). He was also a member of the Norwegian Male Chorus and Leif Erikson Lodge No. 1. The Lodge, largely with Mr. Kvalheim at the helm, was responsible for the birth of NORSE HOME. His survivors at the time of his death were his wife, Sigrid, a daughter, two sons and two brothers, one of whom lived in Norway. Abraham's nephew, Trygve Kvalheim, would assume the NORSE HOME presidency in the 1980s.

Abraham O. Kvalheim, known as the "Father of NORSE HOME," died with his boots on, so to speak, at age seventy-three. He collapsed at Norway Center near Seattle's Denny Way during a meeting. His legacy has endured.

FRODE FRODESEN (1882-1966)

Up to this point, discussions about the future NORSE HOME were brief and informal. With the nation in the grip of the Great Depression, the Sons of Norway Lodge No. 1 doggedly urged that steps be taken to establish a retirement home. In an undated document, a reference is made to the "First Meeting" of the "Old Folks Home Committee," which was appointed by Frode Frodesen, President. At the Lodge's December 1932 meeting, Frodesen asked three members to proceed with an effort for the establishment of a home for the aged.

Those members, with Abraham Kvalheim at the helm, met on January 18, 1933. They stated that the idea of a home "should be carried to a conclusion." The Committee also asked for authority to contact other Lodges in Sons of Norway District No. 2, and request their cooperation in establishing a home. Next, the Kvalheim Committee asked for authorization to incorporate.

On March 8, 1933, the Committee resolved that a letter be sent to Lodges in Washington, Idaho, Oregon, British Columbia, and California "north of but including the Lodge at Oakland" requesting each appoint a member to the "old folks committee."

FOR THE RECORD

Because this is a history, it's important to understand the progression of events leading to the founding of NORSE HOME. Following is a listing of meetings and decisions related to the project, 1933-1945. What comes through these tracings, and remains with the reader, is the unrelenting determination of individuals over considerable odds to establish what would eventually become NORSE HOME, an outstanding Retirement Community.

The next large jump was taken on July 30, 1933. The following details are found in the early notes of Cjermunn Dahl, Treasurer of the home Committee. Dahl hosted a gathering (and picnic) of Committee members at his cabin at Lake Goodwin. Representatives from the following Lodges attended: Number 21 Bellingham, Washington (Kasper Aagard); Number 47 Bend, Oregon (Conrad Braaten); Number 5 Spokane, Washington (Sivert Gunderson); and Abraham Kvalheim, Gjermann Dahl and Albert S. Ryland from Leif Erikson Lodge Number 1 Seattle, Washington. Dahl also notes the presence of C.K. Anderson, President of Sons of Norway District Number 2, and E.B. Hauke, Grand Lodge Vice-President, Order of Sons of Norway. The group issued a statement that their work "must be carried on until (a) suitable home is built." Abraham Kvalheim was elected President, and Sivert Gunderson Secretary.

Just before the July 30 meeting at Lake Goodwin, the idea of a retirement home had been raised with the Sons of Norway Supreme Lodge in Minneapolis. The Supreme Lodge opposed the idea, noting that because the Pacific Coast District of the Lodge extended from Mexico to Canada, a home for this entire area would be impractical. According to Dr. T.W. Buschmann, who would become the second President of NORSE HOME (after Abraham Kvalheim), members of the Leif Erikson Lodge nevertheless "decided that a home should be built," and a Committee was authorized to invite "all the lodges interested" to the Lake Goodwin picnic.

STEERING A PATH

From this point forward the team kept matters on track. For example, at the important July 30, 1933, meeting at Lake Goodwin, Mr. Ryland reported on "preliminary work" of the Committee, including a plan of organization and proposed Articles of Incorporation.

The time and thought invested in early planning is clear and extensive. Several Resolutions evolved, changed or were later dropped (noted in changes reflected in the Minutes below). An important decision: At this meeting the Daughters of Norway were invited to join the project on an equal basis with the founding Sons of Norway.

RESOLUTIONS PASSED AT THE JULY 30 MEETING:

1. Every Lodge desiring membership in the Old Folks Home shall make [an] initial contribution of $1.00 for each member in good standing, and thereafter an annual contribution of $.50 per member in good standing.

2. All Lodges making contribution [are] entitled to one representative in the Old Folks Home Corporation. Lodges having 100 or more members in good standing shall be entitled to one additional representative for the first 100 members and one additional representative for every full 200 members above the first 100.

3. Provisions of resolutions 1 & 2 shall be inserted in and made part of the By-Laws of the Corporation.

4. The home [should] not be a burden on the Lodges; [it] shall be [a] self-sustaining institution built and operated from free and voluntary donations, legacies, devises and bequests, and from payments by its guests.

5. Contributions shall be solicited and accepted from nonmembers as well as members of the order, and nonmembers [will] be fully paying guests.

6. By-Laws to provide that persons making contributions therein stipulated that the Corporation shall be associate members thereof.

7. Contribution Lodges and members shall receive first consideration in the charitable work of the Corporation.

8. No funds shall be expended toward buying, building or operating a home until sufficient means are available to place [the] institution on [a] safe, self-sustaining basis assuring its permanency.

9. Until used for the home, funds [are] to be invested in U.S. obligations and Postal Savings.

10. All officers handling funds [are] to [have] surety bond[s] covering funds fully.

11. Changes in Articles of Incorporation, and in expressed policies of [the] Corporation to be submitted to member Lodges and require approval of 2/3 majority of the Lodges for adoption.

12. This Resolution (12) is the approved Articles of Incorporation. Affairs [are] to be managed by (a) Board of Trustees consisting of such number (but not less than 6) as shall be fixed by By-Laws, and shall be elected annually by and from its representative membership. Authority [is] requested to invite Daughters of Norway to join on [the] same basis as Sons of Norway.

THE NECESSARY NAMES AND DATES

Again, for the record, the following dates are provided to indicate the project's constant and unwavering path of growth (except for the World War II years). What appears to be a bland list of names, times and places also reveals unceasing efforts by Sons of Norway to establish NORSE HOME.

- December 13, 1933: The draft Articles of Incorporation is approved, signed, and to be filed with the Secretary of State as soon as possible. (The Secretary of State's office reflects a date of December 10, 1933, when papers were filed. Perhaps these steps were virtually simultaneous.) All members of the Committee representing Lodges were appointed as Trustees for a term ending in February 1934. Their names: Kaspaer Aagaard, Conrad Braaten, Gjermunn Dahl, Sivert Gunderson, Abraham Kvalheim and Albert S. Ryland.

- April 2, 1934: The first meeting is held of the Sons of Norway "Home Corporation." Abraham Kvalheim is elected Chair pro tem; Albert S. Ryland, Secretary pro tem. Four Lodges elected representatives to the Corporation. Other members were O.O. Hvatum, Gjermunn Dahl, and Conrad Braaten.

- May 6, 1934: A bank (unnamed but apparently Peoples Bank and Trust Co.) is chosen to deposit funds; bond for a Treasurer is approved; payment for costs of incorporation is approved.

- June 24, 1934: At the Annual Meeting it is resolved that a pamphlet be prepared, printed and distributed about the home. Life Membership is established at $50, with Associate memberships at $1.00 per year.

- September 23, 1934: By-Laws are approved and it is adopted that seed money from the Leif Erikson Lodge Number 1 be loaned to the Building Committee, with a promissory note issued by the Treasurer.

- November 18, 1934: Trustees met with the Lutheran Welfare Committee regarding the possibility of joining forces to erect the home. It was concluded that such a partnership is not practical nor in the best interest of the cause (no details given).

- (NOTE: During this period the Board employed Kornelius Johnson, an early supporter of the project in 1929, to solicit funds for the building. According to A.S. Ryland, Secretary pro tem, Johnson "collected several thousand dollars of which Norwegian Consul Einar Beyer contributed the first thousand.")

- March 27, 1935: Pamphlet is approved. The Treasurer is authorized to "form clubs" to work for the project. An expenditure of $25 is authorized for the services of "Mrs. Benson" in the organization of "clubs."

- December 9, 1936: Secretary is authorized to draw up amendment (unspecified) to By-Laws providing new basis for Lodges to become members of the Corporation.

- April 16, 1937: Resolution is passed to engage an individual (unnamed) to solicit funds for the home project.

- June 19, 1937: By-laws changed to admit Lodges of Daughters of Norway and to reduce financial requirements for membership. (According to one document, the June 19 meeting was adjourned to July 30, 1937. The reason given was "in order to give the Daughters of Norway Lodges time to consider… whether or not to join.")

- August 30, 1937: The name is officially changed from Sons of Norway Home to NORSE HOME, INC.

- September 11, 1937: Any member who pledges in writing to contribute $5.00 or more to the home shall be considered a sustaining member, and shall have a vote.

- October 5, 1937: Three Trustees (unnamed) selected for varying terms. Arrangements made with Peoples Bank and Trust Co. to accept subscriptions. The Secretary is instructed to write the Leif Erikson and Valkyrien Lodges requesting that they "pick up their notes due the NORSE HOME, INC."

- December 16, 1937: Resolved: To secure an option on "Lebanon Home property and 9 adjoining lots." (Lebanon Home was originally established in 1908 at 1500 Kilbourne Street, Ballard, as a rescue shelter for homeless girls and women. It later had two other addresses and eventually became a residence for aged and convalescent patients. Its last address, and presumably the site that interested NORSE HOME founders, was at 12th Avenue NW and NW 90th Street, Crown Hill/Ballard.)

- February 3, 1938: Thor C. Tollefson (later a member of the U.S. Congress from Tacoma, Washington) filed re-written Articles of Incorporation with the Secretary of State. For some reason, the State Archives also indicates the incorporation date as February 2, 1938.

What Tollefson filed with the State of Washington:

The *SUPPLEMENTAL ARTICLES OF INCORPORATION*

Article I.
   The name of this corporation shall be and is hereby changed to: "The NORSE HOME, INC."

Article II.
   The location and chief place of business of the corporation shall be in the City of Seattle, King County, Washington.

Article III.

The purpose for which the corporation is formed is to establish, maintain and operate a home or homes for the aged, infirm, indigent, and others in need thereof, and otherwise to carry on the work of benevolence, charity, social welfare and relief, and to do generally any and all things necessary, proper and convenient for the accomplishment of these purposes; and in addition thereto, to have all the general powers granted to like corporations by the laws of the State of Washington.

Article IV.

The corporation shall have no capital stock, but shall consist of representative and sustaining members. The representative membership shall be composed of duly elected representatives from regularly charted lodges in good standing of (1) The Order of Sons of Norway, a fraternal organization organized under the laws of the State of Minnesota, (2) of the Daughters of Norway of the Pacific Coast, a sororal corporation organized under the laws of the State of Washington, and (3) of any fraternal corporation that may be formed by union and amalgamation of the aforementioned corporations. Every lodge in said fraternal organizations which shall comply with the By-Laws of this corporation shall be entitled to elect such number of representative members as said By-Laws shall provide.

All persons who make such financial contribution to the corporation as shall be required in the By-Laws shall be sustaining members of the corporation.

Article V.

The affairs of this corporation shall be managed by a Board of Trustees... etc.

THE 1957 SUPPLEMENT TO THE ARTICLES OF INCORPORATION

The Supplement added powers to: "construct, operate, maintain and improve, and to buy, own, sell, convey, assign, mortgage or lease any real estate and any personal property." It also empowered the corporation to borrow money, have capital stock, and notes several other business and financial details. Most of the changes anticipated Board investments and the purchase of property for NORSE HOME.

FINDING A SITE

Without missing a beat, the Committee continued its search for a site. After rejecting the Lebanon Home property (December 16, 1937, above), and after briefly considering buying the Burlingame Hotel on Seattle's traditional Capitol Hill in 1951 (discussed in the following chapter), the original 1938 property site on Phinney Ridge remained the prime and eventually only location.

Curiously, as late as 1952 and long after purchase of the Phinney Ridge property, the Board took a look at the old Children's Orthopedic Hospital building on Queen Anne Hill. In fact, an offer was made to purchase the property for $250,000, later raised to $400,000. The offer was not accepted. Later, realtors informally told Dr. Buschmann that the hospital thought it could get $700,000-$800,000 for the hospital and its land. The matter was dropped by NORSE HOME leaders and full attention was again given to the Phinney Ridge property.

The site at 5301 Phinney Avenue North, tax parcel 952310-0630, was acquired by NORSE HOME, Inc. on January 23, 1938, from the estate of Paul Noglebert et al on a real estate contract (volume 1789 of deeds, page 11). A deed was issued on September 6, 1939, to the NORSE HOME, INC., from O.S. Haugen (volume 1859 of deeds, page 650).

Although the purchase was for "a portion" of block 72 of the Woodland Park Addition Supplement, the remainder of the parcel — a complete city block — was eventually obtained. (It is unclear whether this parcel — the present site of NORSE HOME — was once owned by Guy Phinney.)

THE EARLY PATH

- March 29, 1938: Resolved: To offer $600 or more (not to exceed $7,000) for a block located between North 53rd and North 54th Streets and Phinney and Greenwood Avenues (the current site of NORSE HOME). The Treasurer is instructed to close the deal. Another source indicates this tract of land may have been found by NORSE HOME supporters as early as 1933.

- May 4, 1938: Treasurer is instructed to close the deal on the Phinney property for $6,500.

- July 19, 1938: The NORSE HOME Corporation is made residuary legatee of the estate of John Ericson of Denver, Colorado. Value: about $2,000. The Treasurer is authorized to borrow money to make payment on the Phinney property.

- NOTE: Mr. Ryland asserts that "before and after the (Phinney) site was purchased, various propositions were submitted to the Board to purchase sites with complete buildings more or less suitable for the Home." A number of admonitions and suggestions were also received. All these issues were carefully examined and turned down. Chapter: NORSE HOME, CALL TO ACTION

PROPERTY IN HAND

- August 16, 1938: A form letter is sent to Lodges of the Sons and Daughters of Norway urging them to join the home Corporation.

- September 10, 1938: Annual Meeting. Elections are held to fill vacancies on the Board of Trustees.

- September 15, 1938: Resolved: To carry on an intensive campaign for funds. Cost of the campaign is "not to exceed 10% unless meals [are] furnished workers." President (Abraham Kvalheim) and two other directors served as supervisors of the campaign.

- October 7, 1938: Thelma Lodge Number 26, Everett, Washington, withdrew from the project. Membership of the Board of Trustees is increased to fifteen.

- November 4, 1938: Knute Rockne Lodge, Seattle, Washington, and Sverre Lodge, Aberdeen, Washington, joined the Corporation.

- January 7, 1939: Resolved: To pay transportation costs for Board Members from points "outside Seattle."

- March 11, 1939: Approval of a circular for the campaign.

- January 11, 1940: The Estate of Soren G. Halvorsen ($4,000) is willed to the Corporation.

- February 4, 1949: Annual Meeting is held. Delegates from seven lodges are present, along with 40 sustaining members. Four Trustees are elected (unnamed). Resolved: 1. NORSE HOME funds to be paid only on vouchers signed by the President and Secretary; 2. Books will be audited every six months; 3. Approval to hire a campaign manager.

- February 12, 1940: Contract is approved with Pierce-Hedrick, Inc. for $3,000 to conduct the campaign over a period of fifteen weeks. Mr. C.K. Warne of Pierce-Hedrick was put in charge.

- March 10,1940: Resolved: To elect seven members to the Committee in addition to the president and secretary.

EUROPEAN INTERRUPTIONS

The invasion of Norway on April 9, 1940, was a blow to Norwegians everywhere. Other nationalities, especially with Scandinavian roots, were resentful and indignant. The attack focused on major Norwegian ports (Narvik, Trondheim, Bergen, Kristiansand, Oslo). Germany claimed that by invading Norway it would forestall British actions in Scandinavia and the Baltic Sea.

Leif Terdal, in his 2008 book, *Our Escape from Nazi-Occupied Norway*, relates the following: "I am still disturbed by the memory of seeing German soldiers marching past our house with rifles and military vehicles and knowing that my mother was outraged by their presence. One day, when I was about four years old, as I was alone playing in our front yard, I paused to watch about twenty soldiers march past carrying weapons. I picked up a stone and threw it at them. I later told my mother. She scolded me severely."

Seattle's large patriotic Norwegian contingent was shocked by news from the Old Country. A national relief effort was immediately launched. Clothing, money, food and medicine were sent to Norwegian recipients through Sweden and Denmark.

The campaign to build a Seattle home for the elderly came to an abrupt halt. Funds and attention were turned immediately to the European homeland. Yet, the campaign Committee did not fold its tent. It only dropped the flap for several years.

Shortly after the defeat of Germany the campaign was reinvigorated. Constitution Day (May 17) celebrations and seasonal dinners and bazaars were organized. Funds were re-generated by the campaign, although lines of support to Norway continued for some time.

- January 6, 1940: Lyngblomsten Lodge joins Corporation. Officers of Corporation instructed to request a rezoning of west 70 feet of NORSE HOME property.

- April 16,1940: Resolve: To make the NORSE HOME fund campaign secondary to Aid to Norway.

- November 10, 1940: Annual Meeting. Assets of $27,000 reported. New Officers of Board elected (unnamed). Authorization is given to publish a "small monthly bulletin re NORSE HOME" for public distribution.

- January 11, 1941: A monthly bulletin called NORSE HOME Review is produced. Resolved: To form "Ladies Guilds" (later organized and guided by Inga Frodesen).

- May 20, 1941: A new Committee is designated to undertake financial aspects of project.

- 1941: Abraham O. Kvalheim, after ten years as president, declined to stand for re-election. Dr. T.W. Buschmann was elected president. After the Committee's assets reached over $200,000, it began the search for architects and contractors who could put the NORSE HOME dream on paper.

DR. T.W. BUSCHMANN (1888-1973)

Memories and documents about Dr. T.W. Buschmann's long association with NORSE HOME were shared in an interview with his daughter and son-in-law, David and Helen Belvin, and their daughter, Ilene Garland, in 2011.

Dr. Trygve W. Buschmann's older brother, August (mentioned several times in subsequent chapters), wrote a 1960 piece for Alaska Sportsman describing his family's love affair with Alaska. In fact, his story is titled "I Grew up with the North."

AUGUST BUSCHMANN (1880-1964)

The Buschmann family, which included eight children (one more sibling was born in the United States), emigrated from Norway to America in 1891. Tacoma, Washington, became the family's temporary home. After establishing a seafood saltery in Port Townsend, Washington, Peter Thams Buschmann did the same at Fairhaven (Bellingham) and on Lummi Island. An early visit by Peter and son August to Ketchikan, Alaska, led to a lifetime devotion to the Great Land. Peter and his sons, over many years, established a number of Alaska canning, salting and icing ventures. The picturesque town of Petersburg at the north end of Wrangell Narrows, which later became the "halibut capital of the world," was named for Peter Buschmann.

After Peter died in 1903, August and his brothers Christian Henrik, Eigil and Leif continued to run or establish family businesses in Petersburg, Bartlett Cove (Glacier Bay), Sitkoh Bay in Peril Straits, Taku Inlet, Icy Straits, Kenai River, and elsewhere. Although younger brother Trygve worked at family canneries and other operations during vacation, he had his eye on a different career. After high school he received a medical degree from the University of Pennsylvania in 1913. His long career as a physician and surgeon was spent in Seattle, Washington. During the later years of his practice, Dr. T.W. Buschmann devoted almost fifteen years as board member or president of NORSE HOME, INC., later named NORSE HOME. His downtown Seattle office, rooms 629-638 in the Stimson Building, became the unofficial headquarters of the NORSE HOME project, including planning, record keeping, fund raising and management.

WAR YEARS

For almost three years the NORSE HOME campaign was dormant. Noted above, personal and financial resources were directed toward winning a two-front war (Pacific and European theaters). Special concern and help was also directed toward the plight of German-occupied Norway. World War II superseded everything in Seattle and throughout America. Despite the suspension of overt activities, the Sons and Daughters of Norway and other supporters did not forget their goal: establishing a home for the aged on Phinney Ridge. For example, toward the end of the War several meetings related to NORSE HOME were held.

- October 3, 1943: Annual Meeting was held with 50 sustaining members and delegates present. Eight NORSE HOME Guilds were represented and reported cash and bonds on hand in excess of $1,500. New Board officers were elected. Also, Resolved: 1. Prepare Life

Membership certificates; 2. Acknowledgement of the primary purpose of NORSE HOME: i.e., caring for the "aged and infirm." In that regard, the Board intends to "make the home a general central service in the welfare of our people. Single persons having no home [can] be provided with facilities for storage of personal effects and mail handling if desired."

- February 11, 1944: Resolved: To convert the estate of John Ericson to cash (see July 19, 1938, above).

- June 5, 1944: Organization of a Committee of 100 men to help raise $150,000. Before shaping a coordinated professional fund raising effort, several unusual approaches were used to reach the general public. One example: An advertisement was placed in a Seattle newspaper, which included a Biblical reference. Luke 2:7 was quoted: "There was no room for them in the inn," followed by "Is there no room in our hearts for these old friends? There can be room… there WILL be room… Let your heart decide just how much… Do it Now!" Another similar advertisement used the quotation: "Greater Love Hath No Man — Than To Lay Down His Life For His Friend."

Following the end of World War II, the 1945 Annual Meeting focused on "methods of maintaining interest of [the] public in NORSE HOME, and solicitation of funds."

DR. BUSCHMANN'S CREDO

In a 1941 interview, Dr. T.W. Buschmann described the rationale for NORSE HOME. His words can be interpreted as a heartfelt reason for looking after one's parents and grandparents and as an informal philosophy of NORSE HOME:

"… each and every one of us, whether a lodge member or not, has an obligation to the aged. Most of these old people are honest, upright, hard-working individuals who have toiled faithfully at manual labor throughout the best period of their lives, and in spite

thereof, in many instances are unable to provide comfortably for themselves in their declining years. The success and financial status of many of us are directly or indirectly the result of the labor of these individuals. We who have benefitted from their labor and toil owe it to them to do what we can for their comfort and happiness in their old age."

Dr. Buschmann responded to three objections to the construction of NORSE HOME:

1. The enactment of Social Security has made a home unnecessary. Answer: Elder citizens often live in unpleasant circumstances, and frequently their environment is lacking the "association and companionship which means so much to these old people."

2. Retirement homes are costly. Answer: NORSE HOME was not built until sufficient funds were in hand and "the only expense to the guests will be the cost of operation."

3. Uncertainties of World War II (Dr. Buschmann wrote these comments in 1941). Answer: Never has the country as a whole enjoyed such a boom as we are now witnessing. The average wage earner has never been better paid. Business has never been better than at present."

THEIR OWN LIVES

While NORSE HOME planning and fundraising were underway, ANNA and HARALD LARSSEN were making their own home in Ballard. Although there were announcements about the new retirement home in both English and Norwegian language newspapers, the descriptions that emerged seemed to outline hopeful concepts and dreams. ANNA had little time to do anything except build her nursing career and marriage — both brand new experiences. HARALD was surrounded by Old Timers, who were watching the new kid as he reached for tools and put his head down at the boat works. Within a few years, a large building would rise on Phinney Ridge. In time, NORSE HOME would attract both ANNA and HARALD.

Bricks and Mortar
The Gold Key

"The President (Dr. T.W. Buschmann)… spoke at length about the work during past years and about the new requirements under the new law governing "old people's" homes and nursing homes. He thereupon called for remarks by some of the out of town representatives and visitors, all of whom expressed themselves in favor of renewed efforts to get the Home built at the earliest possible date."

(Minutes of the 1951 Annual Meeting of NORSE HOME, INC.)

QUERIES AND CONSIDERATIONS

The title of this section is misleading. Bricks were not used in the construction of NORSE HOME. If they had been, NORSE HOME booster and early leader Frode Frodesen would likely have been an important contractor for the project. Anne Marie Frodesen Steiner, Frode's daughter and member of a founding family of NORSE HOME, remembers her father's brick business and his long interest in all aspects of the planned retirement home, including his position as president of the NORSE HOME board.

Before contracts were let to construct NORSE HOME, last-minute questions arose regarding the NORSE HOME Phinney Ridge site. Examples:

Mr. Cassius M. Pettit in Kirkland, Washington, suggested the Board look at a 23.5 acre residential property he owned in the Juanita Point District near Lake Washington. Because of its access to Lake Washington and large acreage, he thought it would yield a good return on the Board's investment. He added that "because of illness" in his family, the offer was for quick sale at a bargain price.

Another issue: An unnamed individual sent an undated note to several members of the Board raising these questions:

1. There will likely be an "extra cost" to construction because of the difference in grade between Phinney and Greenwood Avenues, necessitating a bulkhead;
2. An appropriate entrance to the building must be planned for "delivery of supplies and collection of garbage";
3. Size of the Phinney Ridge property may not be large enough for a proper retirement home.

During the Annual Meeting on March 27, 1955, outgoing President Dr. T.W. Buschmann defended the Board's 1953-1954 decisions to buy stock in Voss Oil Company and Wyton Oil Company. Dr. Buschmann noted, despite "criticism by so many," that favorable returns on these investments have been invested in NORSE HOME.

The above queries were answered by the Board in writing and by its actions.

Dr. Buschmann also observed that there had been criticism of the Board for "not having started the building" at an earlier time. His rebuttal: The money at hand until now was not enough to erect a proper home instead of a "one-story building on the outskirts of town."

"A RETIREMENT COMMUNITY" (a sign at NORSE HOME's main entrance)

Norwegian history has been an integral part of NORSE HOME history. The Norwegian-American writer Odd S. Lovoll believes that the Sons of Norway — principal founders of NORSE HOME — have had the most success in forging a path to Norwegian fraternalism. Creating conditions and facilities for immigrants or the children of immigrants with common interests has long been a modus operandi of this organization.

Serving more or less as an historical template for Seattle's NORSE HOME, Chicago Norwegians spawned an early effort to form a mutual aid society in the 1870s. Perhaps the first successful and lasting contribution to a Norwegian "retirement culture" was by the Sons of Norway in Minneapolis during the 1890s. The Sons of Norway system of lodges established a pattern. Lovoll also asserts that nursing homes do better than hospitals in preserving Norwegian culture. And there is little doubt that the Pacific Northwest-based Sons of Norway traveled the "extra mile" in helping establish NORSE HOME.

Equal billing goes to the Daughters of Norway. The Daughters' first lodge, Valkyrien, was established in 1905 in Seattle. There are more Daughter lodges in Washington than in any other state. Many of the lodges are small — from 50 to 100 members — and older women dominate the rolls. However, Norwegian entertainment and crafts such as rosemaling have attracted younger members. NORSE HOME services and celebrations have also interested women of all ages.

Seattle's NORSE HOME is mentioned in Lovoll's 1998 book, *The Promise Fulfilled*. Illustrating his book title as well as the story of NORSE HOME, Lovoll writes: "… the building and operation of NORSE HOME demonstrate that an appeal on the basis of nationality elicits a charitable response."

A SPECIAL STORY

Norwegian-born Soren G. Halvorsen, 84 years old, died in Seattle on January 4, 1940. Halvorsen had been a cook in mining and railroad camps in Alaska from 1900 until returning to Seattle about 1920. A bachelor with no relatives in the United States, he left his entire estate to NORSE HOME, Inc. "for the assistance, happiness and welfare of old people in an old-folks home." A.S. Ryland, attorney for the estate, said Mr. Halvorsen's gift would total about $4,000. There was no information about how Mr. Halvorsen became familiar with the plans for a Seattle-based home for retired people. At the time of Mr. Halvorsen's death, the campaign to build a home for elder citizens on Phinney Ridge was barely underway. The Halvorsen bequest was among hundreds from relatively obscure, hard-working Norse citizens who responded to a dream.

THE CAMPAIGN

Assets in the NORSE HOME kitty were $27,000 in 1940, the results of an eleven-year effort (1929-1940). The War intervened in 1941, but, as noted, beginning in 1944 the Committee commenced another effort. The restart button was pushed by Dr. T.W. Buschmann. In a letter dated May 1, 1944, he wrote to lodges of the Sons of Norway and made the following points:

1. From the attack on Pearl Harbor (by the Japanese) the NORSE HOME project has been inactive.
2. This is the time to resume efforts to build a home for aged citizens.
3. NORSE HOME is a Sons and Daughters of Norway institution.
4. All lodges are invited to join the effort.
5. In Norway, every city of any size has its home for the aged.
6. Guilds have been formed by local women to support NORSE HOME.
7. The general fund drive was launched last week with a dinner at Seattle's Immanuel Lutheran Church.

The record of fundraising after the War, and until the decision was made to build NORSE HOME, is impressive.

1944	$ 45,154.12
1945	61,400.57
1946	79,388.41
1947	92,855.41
1948	110,273.06
1949	112,269.00
1950	192,421.83
1951	212,702.20

1952	221,640.28
1953	233,442.53
1954	244,826.88
1955	413,052.70

SOLICITING FUNDS

In 1944, NORSE HOME fund raising approaches were enumerated. The step-by-step solicitation effort was published and distributed. Following were suggested rules for the campaign:

1. Don't undertake solicitation efforts alone.
2. Be well informed about NORSE HOME — prospective donors will ask questions.
3. Know something about the prospects.
4. Don't be shy about asking deep pocket prospects for large sums.
5. Show prospects the list of what others have given.

Campaign experts assured solicitation agents that letters preceded their visits to specific individuals. These same professionals suggested that the solicitors themselves make out a pledge card, thereby getting a better feel for the solicitation process.

CHEERLEADING

Dr. T.W. Buschmann treated board members to a steak dinner at Norway Center on December 17, 1951. Architect Ed Mahlum presented a plan for NORSE HOME, which became the main subject of the meeting. Mahlum's plan included a theme suggested by Ole Andreassen, manager of the Norway Center: "Honor Thy Father and Thy Mother." This was followed by C.K. Anderson's "rousing speech" of thanks to August Buschmann, who had led much of the fundraising effort. Then, Abraham Kvalheim, the group's first leader, talked about "the spirit of doing something worthwhile, to leave concrete evidence for posterity to see that 'here lived Norwegians,' adding that we can't do that by just eating ourselves into oblivion."

To maintain momentum, in March of 1953, Dr. Buschmann wrote a letter to the NORSE HOME Guilds suggesting that they (and the Norwegian Hospital Association) be represented on the board. If they agreed with his proposition, he asked them to choose three individuals to be elected by the Guilds and the Association. The Guilds and the Norwegian Hospital Association agreed, and NORSE HOME by-laws were amended on June 25, 1953, as follows: "The affairs of the corporation shall be managed by a Board of Trustees to consist of not less than nine members, one-sixth of which number shall be elected from the NORSE HOME Guilds and one-sixth of which shall be elected by the sustaining members, and two-thirds of which number shall be elected by and from the representative members of Lodges and other Norwegian Organizations."

Cheerleading continued with an entertainment planned at Seattle's Metropolitan Theater for Monday, September 14, 1953, titled "Scandinavian Night." Funds for NORSE HOME would result from ticket sales. The Guilds were asked by Dr. Buschmann to lead the publicity effort and boost ticket sales for the event. (Guilds had already turned over funds to the project as a result of bazaars.)

In 1953, after toasts and thanks were given to the principal founders and supporters, the decision to proceed with building NORSE HOME was finally made.

LEGAL AND TECHNICAL STEPS

Details had to be settled before ground-breaking. NORSE HOME Board attorney Howard A. Hanson and architect Edward K. Mahlum went round and round over several issues.

What might have been a serious interruption arose after trustees asked the city to extend the project by a seventy-foot strip fronting Greenwood Avenue. (Mahlum architects had suggested that the entire building footprint be used.) Several neighbors below (west of) the planned NORSE HOME site petitioned the Seattle City Council citing their opposition to the HOME'S proposed rezoning request.

The petitioners claimed that the construction of a "charity home for the aged" on Greenwood Avenue would "depreciate the value of investments" in nearby properties. The City Planning Commission deferred action on the rezoning request for sixty days after explaining to NORSE HOME representatives that construction could proceed — including the seventy-foot strip — if property owners within 400 feet approved it. A petition was quickly circulated and signed by virtually all nearby neighbors consenting to the project as "a philanthropic home for old people." Besides overcoming this zoning challenge, the latter statement of NORSE HOME'S purpose was a more accurate description than "a charity home for the aged" used by the petitioners.

Another matter pertained to whether NORSE HOME could use "all of block 72 (the current site) extending back from Phinney Avenue a distance of 120 feet for its building use." The Seattle Building Department said that an examination of the records indicated NORSE HOME can proceed to use "all of this 120 feet for its building purposes."

THE BURLINGAME APARTMENT HOTEL

There were several other matters raised, including one in 1951 from August Buschmann regarding the possible eviction of seniors from the Burlingame Apartment Hotel at 404 East Howell Street (Capitol Hill). The old Burlingame was at that time being considered a "place of refuge" for elderly people. The Executive Board described it as a six-story steel and concrete, fireproof building with "73 rental rooms with lavatories." It had a dining room, kitchen and lobby. By arranging a long-term lease with the owner, and after necessary modifications, the Board believed that the Burlingame could be financed from "current resources." In a letter dated June 20, 1951, the NORSE HOME Executive Board believed that the goal of erecting a new building could not then be accomplished, so the Burlingame looked like a reasonable option. However, August Buschmann asked: will (Burlingame) pensioners be entitled to financial assistance from the King County Welfare Department if their income is not sufficient to pay the NORSE HOME minimum rate; will the condition of a person's health deny him entrance to NORSE HOME; and if the neighborhood opposes the project and signs a petition of objection, could they stop the project?

From thin extant files, and reading between the lines of correspondence related to the Burlingame project, it appears that the tasks of evicting people from the old building and making needed internal modifications were daunting prospects and fell short of what had been promised supporters. The Burlingame Apartment Hotel disappears from the record in 1951.

(Briefly, the Board also looked at property near the Burlingame site — 1808 Bellevue Avenue. An Option for Sale was prepared in anticipation of purchasing this site for $32,500. Nothing more came of this matter.)

MAINTAINING MOMENTUM

August and his brother Dr. Trygve Buschmann were a one-two team in planning and raising funds for NORSE HOME. However, on July 3, 1951, shortly after shelving the Burlingame Apartment Hotel option, August wrote his brother a letter in which he seemed to express grave disappointment about the project. First, August outlines his relentless efforts to raise funds. Then he notes that the anticipated results have been paltry. Next he writes that "at my age neither my health nor my resources permit me to continue this work further." Finally, he avers that unless the continuing work (for the fundraising, design and construction phases) can be taken over by the NORSE HOME organization, "I believe the funds on hand should be returned to the donors and the project abandoned."

The record does not include a response from Dr. Buschmann to his brother's letter, but, for whatever reason, August's gloomy phase passed and momentum was resumed.

OTHER CHALLENGES

Several wills leaving funds to NORSE HOME were contested by relatives, a few of whom lived in Norway. Most of these matters were settled amicably.

GROUNDBREAKING AND DEDICATION

On November 17, 1955, construction bids were opened at Norway Center. At that moment enough funds were available to build a kitchen, dining room, heating plant and two residential floors. This relatively meager beginning did not intimidate the NORSE HOME Board of Trustees.

Three weeks later, without hesitation and despite cold wintry weather, a groundbreaking ceremony was held on Phinney Avenue between North 53rd and North 54th Streets at 2:00 PM on December 10, 1955. The principal wielders of shovels — who could barely break the frozen ground — included Dr. Trygve W. Buschmann, former President of NORSE HOME (15 years), Abraham O. Kvalheim, former president and considered the "Father" of NORSE HOME (10 years), and Paul P. Berg, current Board president. August Buschmann, although not an official shoveler, was present along with several patrons and friends of NORSE HOME.

Thor Bjornstad, NORSE HOME's Building Committee Chairman, was in charge of the little ceremony. Dr. H.A. Stub gave the invocation. Other speakers were Mrs. Frode (Inga) Frodesen, known as the "Mother of NORSE HOME" and president of NORSE HOME Guilds, Seattle Mayor Allan Pomeroy, and Norwegian Consul C.A. Stang. As Master of Ceremonies at the chilly event, Bjornstad later wrote that "the program was shortened" and his coordinating role "minimal."

WHO QUALIFIES?

Paul Berg, president of THE NORSE HOME, Inc., after reading articles in *Washington-Posten* that he believed were inaccurate, wrote the following response in December 1956:

> *"The NORSE HOME is intended as a Home for elderly people of this area. It is non-sectarian and open to anyone who is acceptable to the entrance committee after personal interview and careful screening.*

The NORSE HOME was sponsored by some of our pioneer Norwegians years ago, which justified its name, but the funds donated and arranged for have been provided by individuals and companies of all nationalities, and a substantial amount — possibly half of the funds available — have been provided by other than Norwegians who are interested in the welfare of elderly people generally."

ENDLESS DETAILS AND ANOTHER DEDICATION

In November, 1956, Ed Mahlum displayed colored renderings of the six-floor building. Cost estimates for furnishing the building were submitted by Frederick and Nelson and The Bon Marché, well-known Seattle department stores. The Board was then asked to decide whether drapes or Venetian blinds should be used. That matter was turned over to a Board Furniture Committee. It was estimated that the cost of furnishing each room would cost between $475 and $524.

Preparation of a cornerstone was discussed. It was decided to lay the stone on April 6, 1957, over a month before the dedication ceremonies.

During this period the Federal Housing Administration was mentioned. The FHA would later play a key role in financing NORSE HOME (discussed below), with architect Ed Mahlum leading the charge.

In mid-1957, Warren Croston was hired as the first Manager of NORSE HOME (a title later changed to Administrator, and then Executive Director). Mr. Croston had been administrator of the Harris Memorial Hospital in Bremerton, Washington, and at that time was assistant manager of the Methodist Deaconess Hospital in Richland, Washington.

On Sunday, May 26, 1957, a formal dedication was held before an imposing completed building in gentler weather. Thor Bjornstad was again Master of Ceremonies. On that occasion Peter D. Wick of Wick Construction Company opened the front door with a Gold Key. The ceremony included the placing of a cornerstone, the presence of Washington Governor Albert D. Rossellini, and Mary Claverly, Assistant Federal Housing Authority Commissioner from Washington, D.C. Mrs. Claverly

(continued on page 157)

Elie Glaamen, in national dress.
NORSE HOME resident who lived to 102 and donated funds for this history book.

Seattle, Washington
September 7, 1937

Dear Friend:

Two months ago a meeting was held at my home discussing ways and means for erecting a Norwegian Old People's Home in Seattle. A lot of interest has been shown in the matter, and good progress has been made. A corporation, The Norse Home Inc., has been formed, consisting of Lodges of the Sons and Daughters of Norway, and individual sustaining members.

I am anxious to develop a strong sustaining membership for the corporation, which is having its first annual meeting next Saturday, September 11th, at 7:30 P.M. in Norway Hall. At that time the sustaining members are to elect three trustees. I am anxious to have you join as a sustaining member, and trust that you will find it possible to attend. A year's membership costs $5.00.

The goal of the organization is to erect and equip a building in Seattle that would accommodate about thirty people, and donate same for the use of old people of Norwegian extraction, these people to pay their own maintenance. I find this a really worth while project that is being undertaken in the right way, and worthy of your full support.

Please, therefore, do your utmost to be present at the meeting, and bring your friends.

Sincerely,

Einar Beyer.

1937 letter from Einar Beyer, Royal consul of Norway for the State of Washington 1933-1941.

May 22, 1950

Mr. R. H. Bailey
c/o Willapoint Oysters
423 Bell St. Terminal
Seattle, Washington

Dear Mr. Bailey:

I have been requested by the Trustees of the Norse Home, Inc. to assist in the solicitation of substantial donations for the Norse Home of Seattle, which I am pleased to do without remuneration. These donations are deductible in computing your Federal income tax. The Trustees authorized me to advise those who do not already know, that this will be a comfortable, non-profit, non-sectarian, self-sustaining home, principally for the aged of the Northwest and Alaska.

The organization's name does not mean that it will be occupied exclusively by Norwegians or Scandinavians, but merely that eleven or twelve years ago this corporation was organized by Norwegians of the Northwest who realized there was an urgent need for a home of this type and then selected this name.

Solicitation of funds was well under way by 1940. Then the second world war broke out and it became necessary for most Norwegians and Scandinavians, as well as others, to solicit and contribute funds for war and other relief. The Norse Home was temporarily put in the background since relief at that time was the paramount issue.

For several years after the war ended relief was still badly needed, but as soon as possible thereafter the Trustees resumed solicitation of funds, on a more extensive scale and now have almost $200,000.00 in liquid assets, including guaranteed subscriptions, and a beautiful building site, fully paid for, which consists of an entire city block, almost adjoining Woodland Park on the west and commanding an unobstructed view of the Olympic Mountains, part of Puget Sound and a large portion of Seattle. This particular site was chosen by the Trustees many years ago on account of its proximity to our beautiful Woodland Park, the convenience of transportation, and the unobstructed and expansive view. The construction and furnishing of the first unit will cost about $550,000.00.

I am intensely interested in this project because providing a comfortable, sanitary, fireproof home for the aged, with facilities for worship and medical care, not dependent upon State or Federal support, is one of the most worthy projects I can imagine. The older one gets the more one realizes its importance. I am speaking from experience, because I have tried to place older people in homes where they could get proper food and care at a reasonable price and I assure you it is very difficult.

Pages 99-101: Two of many letters written by August Buschmann seeking donations to establish the NORSE HOME between 1950 and 1951.

In addition to its being a worthy cause, it is also a very satisfying way of expressing our appreciation, in a material way, for the many opportunities, benefits and privileges we have had over the years in this, the most wonderful country in the world. The people who will occupy this Home during their last few years have done their duty while able. I consider it a privilege and a pleasure to be helpful in providing this Home for them.

If you and I contribute generously now, the other solicitors and I will, with God's help, do the work required to raise the necessary additional funds, in a comparatively short time so the construction of this much-needed home may commence soon. When completed, it will be a credit to the community, to its sponsors, and to you, whose generous contributions will make possible the carrying out of this project - an accomplishment which will give us all life-long satisfaction.

Sincerely,

August Buschmann

This is a worth while project and if you can help me I will be grateful. Can call and give you more particulars if desired.
A.B.

Not just now

August Buschmann
377 Colman Building
Seattle 4, Washington
Elliott 5029

June 14, 1956

Mr. O. L. Ejde
Washington Posten
Fourth and Pike, Seaboard Building
Seattle, Washington

Dear Mr. Ejde:

I have been asked by you and many others why I am willing to devote so much time to help finance the building of the Norse Home, and make substantial donations and other sacrifices for its benefit. I am, therefore, pleased to enumerate below a few of the principal reasons.

I came here from Norway with my parents over sixty-five years ago, landing in Tacoma on June 7, 1891. Father had met with reverses before leaving Norway and decided that America offered a better future, not only for himself but also for his eight children. Upon our arrival here, father told me he had very little money. All of us who were able and old enough immediately went to work. My older brother and I earned our first money selling newspapers, The Tacoma News, on the streets of Tacoma. We have all made a good living, each in his own way, and have been able to save a little through the years; and today those of us who are left are healthy, active and happy.

For this I am very grateful and feel indebted to this area and country for the privileges and comforts my family and I have enjoyed during these many years. I am also grateful to many of my former employees whose important practical ideas and untiring labors were partly responsible for what success I had while active in business, and sincerely hope some of them, if interested, will be able to avail themselves of the suitable accommodations and life security for elderly people the Norse Home has to offer. I have always worked and have done my little bit, as have most others, donating moderately to worthy projects and organizations that are operated principally for the benefit of the community in which I live.

The older I get, the more I appreciate what it means to be a citizen of the United States of America and permitted to live here where we can all enjoy our precious free enterprise system and also share our many advantages with those who are not citizens. One cannot help comparing this privilege with the pitiful conditions prevailing in many parts of the world.

Some years ago I tried to provide fairly comfortable living quarters for several elderly people who were deserving but had little money. After answering dozens of attractive advertisements and making many calls and inquiries, I commenced to realize

Pages 102-103: Purchasers Policy for 5311 Phinney Ave North.

WASHINGTON TITLE INSURANCE COMPANY

SEATTLE, WASHINGTON
CAPITAL $1,350,000

PURCHASER'S POLICY

AMOUNT $ 6500.00   PREMIUM $ 52.50   POLICY No. B-132169

For value, WASHINGTON TITLE INSURANCE COMPANY, hereinafter called the company, a corporation incorporated under the laws of the State of Washington and duly authorized by the State Insurance Commissioner to insure titles, does hereby insure, subject to the annexed conditions, hereby made a part of this policy,   THE NORSE HOME INC.,

representatives (if a corporation, its successors) and assigns, hereinafter called the insured, against loss or damage not exceeding -

SIXTY-FIVE HUNDRED - Dollars,

which the insured may sustain by reason of any defect in the title of   O. S. HAUGEN, whose

true name is O. S. Hougen, as Executor under the last will and

testament of Paul Nogelberg, Deceased,

hereinafter referred to as the seller, to all the estate or interest in the premises specified and described in Schedule A, hereto annexed and hereby made a part of this policy, or by reason of liens or encumbrances charging the same, at the date of this policy, save and except this policy does not insure against loss or damage by reason of any estate or interest, defect, lien, encumbrance or objection noted in annexed Schedule B, which is a part hereof. Any loss under this policy is to be established in the manner provided in said conditions and shall be paid upon compliance by the insured with and as prescribed in said conditions, and not otherwise.

IN WITNESS WHEREOF, the company has caused these presents to be authenticated by the facsimile signatures of its President and its Manager respectively, lithographed hereon, and its corporate seal to be affixed; but this policy is not valid unless attested by a Vice-President, the Secretary or an Assistant Secretary.

Dated this   5th   day of   May,   19 38 , at   eight o'clock   A. M.

WASHINGTON TITLE INSURANCE COMPANY

L. S. Booth
President.

Charlton L. Hall
Manager.

Attest:

J. A. Nagl
Assistant Secretary.

Aerial view of zoo and property for future location of NORSE HOME.

1944 *Washington-Posten* ad showing one of the original drawings for the building.

1944 *Washington-Posten* ad to buy Series F War bonds as support for NORSE HOME.

SEC. 562 P. L. & R.

The Norse Home Review

Vol. 1.   BOTHELL, WASHINGTON, MARCH, 1941   Number 1

THE NORSE HOME, INC.

Purpose: To build a Home and Norse center worthy of the Sons and Daughters of Norway.

Site: On Phinney Avenue, overlooking the Sound and Olympics on the west and Woodland Park on the east—an ideal spot for old folks to stroll about and enjoy the beauties of nature.

Labor and self-sacrifice on the part of all concerned will be required to carry this worth-while project through to a successful conclusion, but let us remember that nothing worthwhile is accomplished without effort and the reward of that effort will be a fitting, modern structure providing comfortable surroundings for our old people, relatives, and friends—a place where they may find companionship of their own kind; where they will retain that freedom of action and financial independence so characteristic of our race and thus supplying an environment which will make their declining years a joy and not a curse.

You and I will be glad to visit this Home. Our friends and relatives will be glad to greet us there at their home and we will be proud of the fact that we have done our part to make it possible.

The work of financing the Norse Home, just as any other worthwhile undertaking, will be fraught with many trials and tribulations, but it is sure to bring us into closer fellowship and better un-

(Continued on page 4)

OLD AGE PENSION AND OLD FOLKS' HOMES

The old age pension has removed from the aged the economic distress which the recent depression, unemployment, and changing conditions brought about. The old age pension does not, however, do away with the need of old folks' homes. On the contrary, it has greatly increased the demand for such homes. In former years only those who by good fortune or stringent self-denial could save enough to pay for themselves in advance were able to enter such homes. Now these homes are open to all.

So long as an old person is well and able to care for himself, he can make his home anywhere. But when the aged become feeble and unable properly to care for themselves, the need for homes becomes urgent. Only those of very large means who can employ ample help then remain independent. Others who have to depend upon their children or other relatives or friends for their care become worried and unhappy, feeling that they are a burden.

The recent instance of the old mother leaving a note, "You will find my body when the tide is out," and then wading into Puget Sound, was an extreme case, but there is much unhappiness among the aged because they feel they are a burden and in the way. While the young folks may gladly and without complaint care for

(Continued on page 3)

ST. OLAF COLLEGE

The largest and best known Norwegian-American educational institution, St. Olaf College, Northfield, Minnesota, has now let the contract for a new library building which for some time has been very much needed. The cost will be $312,000, nearly all of which has been contributed by graduates and former students of St. Olaf.

The new building will be a beautiful stone structure, in style somewhat like the newer buildings and the library at the University of Washington.

GREETINGS FROM PRESIDENT HAUKE

Editor, "Norse Home Review":

It is with a great deal of appreciation that I am accepting the privilege of contributing my little share to the "Norse Home Review" on the occasion of its initial appearance. A journal of this kind will undoubtedly be of great help to all members of your organization in the collection of funds for "Norse Home" and to keep them informed of its progress. I am very happy that the benevolent and humanitarian hopes and efforts of building an Old Peoples' Home, which originated in Sons of Norway and continued thru your organization, will be carried forward to a successful completion. Altho Sons of Norway found it necessary to discontinue the Old Peoples' Home idea as a part

(Continued on page 2)

1941 *Norse Home Review.*

Preliminary Sketch—The Norse Home

An early drawing of the possible NORSE HOME building.

Norse Home To Be Built Next Year

Ground will be broken for the Norse Home for the aged on April 2, 1950. It will be built between Phinney and Greenwood Avenues on the east and west, and between North 53rd and North 54th Streets on the south and north.

Fine Program Given At Annual Meeting Of Norse Home, Inc.

On Sunday, October 30, at 2 p. m., about 200 people met in the P.-I. Auditorium for the annual meeting of the Norse Home, Inc.

Dr. T. W. Buschmann presided and a splendid program was given. Gov. Arthur B. Langlie spoke of the need of homes for the aged in the State of Washington and pointed out that only love can build such homes. "Nowhere in the city of Seattle could you have found a better location than the one you selected," the governor said. "The beauty of the sunset will surely give the right atmosphere to many lovable aged people and make them happy in the sunset of their lives.

"Yes, such homes are needed," the governor continued, "and the Scandinavian people always have been the most progressive in this country. Now they are leading the way again with this splendid monument."

Miss Jean Douglas gave violin solos and Miss Betty Anderson sang Norwegian folk melodies, attired in national costume. Mrs. Gladys Haug accompanied. Reports from the 16 guilds were given, also reports from the board. Dr. T. W. Buschmann, president of the board, reported a steady gain of interest, while Treasurer Jacob Samuelsen reported the building fund sum. Breaking of ground will take place on April 2, 1950.

The home will be built on a plot bordered by N. 53rd and N. 54th Sts., and Phinney and Greenwood Aves.

Reelected president was Dr. T. W. Buschmann. Other members of the board are: A. S. Ryland, secretary; John Schau, recording secretary; Jacob Samuelsen, treasurer; Kasper Aagaard; trustees, are August Buschmann, Dr. T. W. Buschmann, Mrs. Inga Frodesen, Harold J. Gangmark, A. Kvalheim, Mrs. Bergliot Miller, Mrs. Haldis Sandnes, Fred Fredricksen, Capt. John Skarpness, Sivert Gunderson, Alfred Ostness, George Wold, Mrs. Lena Holland, Mrs. Anna Satre and T. Overby.

Architect Edv. Mahlum gave a splendid report and fine information concerning the building.

1949 *Seattle PI* ad showing yet a new drawing of the potential NORSE HOME, indicating ground breaking planned for Oct of 1950, (which did not happen).

Norse Home, Model For All of U.

Thirty years in the making, Seattle's $1,200,000 Norse Home is a saga of Norwegian perseverance that culminated in an eleventh-hour fight for national legislation to help make the dream come true. It took a lot of effort from its tireless backers, and then some from topnotch Washington politicos, to pull the project over the last big hump. And by a curiously fated coincidence Norse Home also became the model retirement home on which a brand new FHA loan-guarantee policy is being patterned throughout the United States.

All six stories of the Home on Phinney avenue, between N. 53rd and N. 54th streets, will be ready for occupancy by May or June, Edward Mahlum, the architect, estimates. But recently, a critical stage in financing the project was averted only in the last moment.

The slambang finale reads like the last act of a melodrama. Remember?—the heroine faints in the villain's deadly clutch. Some Viking heroes — Norse Home officials, Governor Langlie, Senators Jackson and Magnuson—stepped in for the rescue. Then like the old U.S. army cavalry aiding pioneers of yore, some needed federal assistance arrived in the nick of time to reward the efforts of that rescue mission. The reward: FHA insurance of Norse Home mortgages.

Norse Home then pressed on for more "justice." Mahlum met with FHA officials and was among those that requested the President to permit use of a special fund to aid housing built by non-profit corporations exclusively for the aged. The president agreed in the heat of the campaign — to the tune of $20,000,000. The Home should get its fair share of that "prize money."

Norse Home Inc. is a non-profit corporation, sponsored by Norwegian lodges, organizations and individual sustaining members in Seattle and vicinity.

The Home will provide "150 acceptable, ambulatory persons 65 and over each with a double bedroom" and the most modern facilities of a model home for the aged—plus an infirmary. Each bedroom, measuring 12 feet by 15 feet, will include a full bathroom, large closet, telephone and TV

Federal Housing Administration works out rules and regulations for building of homes for the aged, with the Seattle project as a perfect model

Edward Mahlum, Architect

struction is completed.

Norse Home states that an accepted applicant may pay for accommodations by:

"1. Payment of a minimum of $90 per month for board and care. This plan is on a month-to-month basis. Social security or state welfare funds may be used to supplement private funds for the monthly payments.

"2. By the payment of 'founder's fee'; in other words, selecting and paying for the use of a room. Residents paying a minimum founder's fee of $5,500 will be assured of a private room with bath for the rest of their lives. In addition, monthly payments for board and care must be made.

"3. Payment of a fee in cash or its equivalent, acceptable to the board, at the time entering the Home. The amount of the fee may vary with the age and state of health of the applicant. Under this plan, no further payment is re-

"From 30 to 50 rooms may be reserved for people who are unable to pay the founder's fee," says Mahlum. "However, that will be contingent upon the Home's financial standing and the amount of donations from charitable people by the time it's in operation. The Home will cater mainly to people of moderate means. According to percentage estimates of deaths, about seven or eight percent of the rooms may be resold each year. The construction loan may be amortized in a period of 20-30 years."

Six years ago, the Norse Home project, then only on paper, was temporarily postponed due to the difficulty of raising funds through private donations. August Buschmann, a stalwart in this undertaking along with Abraham Kvalheim, who helped pioneer the project many years ago, invested in a prospective oil well. Buschmann induced fellow-Norwegian backers of Norse Home to do likewise. The

they would have to mal the loss.

The deal paid off ha The group netted $200, the sale of their stock in and Norse Home Inc. denly endowed with a gr of $300,000 in cash. W funds, a new board, h Paul Berg, was elected 1954 and launched a new the undertaking. Constru gan December 6, 1955.

Mahlum and Buschmar the forefront of the car press for legislative act: could aid projects lik Home. They actively eng Senators Jackson and M all the state's congress Governor Langlie to seel tion. A pending house bil: federal long-term loans building of housing for But it had been tabled ir committee.

"We told Jackson, Pell and others to move he earth, if need be, to get tion on that bill," says Then another bill with a provision was passed th last day before adjournn result, non-profit org can now obtain FHA ins mortgages on housing building for the aged."

Three high FHA offic to Seattle this fall t Norse Home while prepa lations for the new poli

"The FHA measure President's decision give Home a green light all Mahlum concludes. "An clears the way for oth projects to proceed 'f ahead.'"

Perhaps the high-mi poses which energized I backers to work withou gain, was an even gre than the efforts made federal aid. Without tl and the good cooperati board, Norse Home wo failed long ago.

Happily it also appea played some part in pror growing national con America's 14,000,000 age Certainly, Norse Home as a local monument t of meeting the challenge citizens present to Ame —Thor Nyman.

Picture and article of Mr. Ed Malhum, architect of NORSE HOME.

AT THE GROUND-BREAKING CEREMONY...

DECEMBER 10, 1955,

NORWEGIAN CONSUL C. A. STANG said:
"It is traditional with Norwegians to adequately take care of the aged . . . "

NORSE HOME PRESIDENT PAUL P. BERG:
"The new board elected last April was given a mandate to proceed with the construction of the Home and promises of help . . . We now have started and call on your help . . . "

NORSE HOME GUILD PRESIDENT,
MRS. F. FRODESEN:
"We will all be so happy when we can think of this lovely Home and know that our old are receiving good and loving care . . . "

DR. H. A. STUB, PASTOR OF
IMMANUEL LUTHERAN CHURCH:
"There is a great need for both the Norse Home and the L. C. Foss Sunset Home . . . "

DR. T. W. BUSCHMANN, Immediate
Past President:
"With the $400,000 collected in the past and with the loyal support of everyone, we will build the entire building. . . . It is sorely needed . . . "

PRESIDENTS BUSCHMANN—KVALHEIM—BERG

and ABRAHAM KVALHEIM, "The Father of Norse Home" and its first president:
"After all these years . . . to see the Home started . . . makes me feel that my life may not have been all in vain . . . "

Who Are the Principal Supporters of the Home?

You, and the other generous, humanitarian, civic-minded Norwegian-American citizens of this community, Washington and Alaska, who appreciate our old-timers and wish to have a part in this great undertaking for them. Your initial support will enable the erection of the building and after its completion the monthly payments by the residents plus anticipated gifts and legacies from our sponsoring members will cover the actual cost of operations.

How can you help the Home? There is no end to the needs—as the needs increase with the numbers of the aged. And there is no end to the help you can provide, thereby insuring a happy ending to the story of all who will come to the Home seeking care, shelter and contentment.

YOU CAN HELP the future development of the Home and its services by remembering the Home with a bequest in your will.

YOU CAN HELP develop needed special facilities now by establishing a Memorial to a dear departed relative or friend.

YOU CAN HELP maintain the residents of the Home with a gift in Honor of a loved one.

YOU CAN HELP in many ways — ways in which you can make a gift to the Home and *still* be *thrifty* in your generosity. Your attorney will be happy to point out in greater details the savings and tax advantages of a gift by you to The Norse Home, Inc.

THE NORSE HOME FINANCE COMMITTEE
INVITES YOUR WHOLEHEARTED SUPPORT *Now!*

Please bring or send your contribution to the Finance Committee, The Norse Home, Inc., 300 Third Avenue West, Seattle 99, Washington.

ALF LARSEN, *Chairman.*

"LA OSS SAMFUNNET TRYGGE — GI FULLT AV VAAR TROHET, VAAR EVNE OG AAND."
From a Poem by Robert Ashton Moen, Dedicated to the Supporters of Norse Home

Pages 111-114: Dec 1955 - At the Ground Breaking Ceremony documents and information

GENERAL INFORMATION ABOUT THE NORSE HOME

THE NORSE HOME is a home for the aged, owned and operated by the Norse Home, Inc., a non-profit corporation.

The Norse Home, Inc., is sponsored by Norwegian lodges, organizations, and individual sustaining members in Seattle and vicinity.

It is governed by a Board of Trustees, at present consisting of 18 members. Twelve of these Trustees are elected from representatives of Norwegian lodges and organizations, three are elected from representatives of the Norse Home Guilds, and three from representatives of the sustaining members.

A Manager, employed by the Board of Trustees, has direct charge of the Home.

The Norse Home is a fireproof, reinforced concrete building, located between Phinney Avenue and Greenwood Avenue and between North 53rd Street and North 54th Street. It has unobstructed view of Ballard, Puget Sound and the Olympic Mountains to the west.

Across Phinney Avenue is Woodland Park, a large, municipally-owned park, zoo, and recreational facilities. This will provide limitless hours of recreation and pleasure for Norse Home residents and their visitors.

Any acceptable ambulatory person over 65 years of age is eligible to become a resident of the Home. A resident who becomes bed-ridden may be retained in the Home to the limit of the facilities.

An accepted applicant in the Norse Home may pay for accommodations by:

1. Payment of a minimum of $90 per month for board and care. This plan is on a month-to-month basis. Social Security or State Welfare funds may be used to supplement private funds for the monthly payments.

2. By the payment of a "Founder's Fee"; in other words, selecting and paying for the use of a room. Residents paying a minimum founder's fee of $5,500.00 will be assured of a private room for the rest of their lives. In addition, monthly payments for board and care to be arranged.

3. Payment of a fee in cash or its equivalent, acceptable to the board, at the time of entering the Home. The amount of the fee will vary with the age and other qualifications of the applicant. Under this plan, no further payment is required during the life of the resident. However, the resident must make additional adequate provisions for surgery, special hospital treatment, if required, and funeral expenses.

The Norse Home anticipates accepting some charity cases. However, since the Home's only income is from residents and donations, and since substantial payments may also be required temporarily for construction costs the Charity cases will depend on the liberal support of those residents, individuals and organizations who can afford to give.

Any unusual situations will be decided by the Board of Trustees.

The information contained herein is the latest and to the best of my knowledge.

ALF LARSEN, *Chairman,*
Finance Committee.

For further information inquire at

THE NORSE HOME, Inc.   300 Third Ave. W.   Phone GA. 1810   Seattle 99, Wash.

THE NORSE HOME **IS** UNDER CONSTRUCTION**!**

The Norwegians of Washington and Alaska have for many years planned on building a home to adequately care for the aged.

The rapid rise in prices charged by present homes has caused local Norwegian lodges, organizations and individuals to get together and start building a Norse Home to furnish better living at half the cost. An excellent location has been purchased, $400,000 has been collected, and construction has started.

Your interest and contributions are now needed to complete the building.

Our dream for a quarter of a century is becoming a reality!

By May 6, 1956, we must decide upon the privilege of accepting the low bid costs for the two additional floors . . . or . . . complete our contract for the basement and two floors, which we all agree are totally inadequate.

VIEW FROM PHINNEY AVENUE

You are invited to visit our site at Phinney Avenue and North 54th Street and

WATCH THE PROGRESS
OF OUR CONTRACTORS

Wick Construction Co.   **Ballard Plumbing & Heating Co.**   **Beckstrom Electric Co.**

How many Old-Timers can Norse Home accommodate?

The fireproof reinforced concrete structure is designed for an ultimate capacity of basement and six floors with

150 TYPICAL DOUBLE BEDROOMS

It is anticipated that most of these will be used as single rooms.

123 ROOMS — Basement and 5 Floors
96 ROOMS — Basement and 4 Floors
69 ROOMS — Basement and 3 Floors
42 ROOMS — Basement and 2 Floors

How many persons we can take care of depend upon our will to succeed. There is need for all six floors.

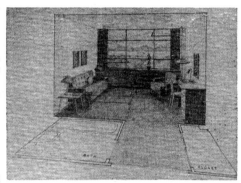

A TYPICAL BEDROOM

is 12' 2" wide, 15' 0" deep with a full bathroom and large closet, has a telephone and TV outlet. Each room can accommodate two persons.

HOW MUCH DOES THE NORSE HOME BUILDING COST?

Contracts were awarded December 6, 1955, for basement and two floors.

Contracts include a six-months' option for the 3rd and 4th floors.

BASEMENT AND 2 FLOORS: $544,006.20—43,140 sq. ft. at $12.61—with 42 bedrooms—84 beds at $6,476.25
BASEMENT AND 3 FLOORS: $666,552.90—55,780 sq. ft. at $11.95—with 69 bedrooms—138 beds at $4,853.06
BASEMENT AND 4 FLOORS: $797,179.74—68,420 sq. ft. at $11.65—with 96 bedrooms—192 beds at $4,099.89

The future 5th and 6th floors if constructed *now* will cost $323,027.77.

All six floors will contain 93,700 sq. ft. at $11.95—with 150 bedrooms—300 beds at $3,733.00

We must assure the financial success of the Home by taking advantage of the good bids and build the most practical and economical operational unit, which is basement and four floors . . . or better still . . . build all six floors.

Pages 115-117: Original NORSE HOME marketing brochure.

VIEW FROM THE NORTHWEST

The Norse Home is located on the sloping hillside west of Woodland Park occupying the entire block bounded by Phinney and Greenwood Avenues, North 53rd and 54th Streets. Across Phinney Avenue to the east, lies Woodland Park. To the west of the building is the garden area, which can be entered directly from the Assembly-Dining Room in the center of the Home.

Th Solariums are located on the southwest corners of the wings, thereby taking advantage of the sun and the view.

The Roof Promenade, which is accessible from the Main Entrance Lobby and the two first-floor Solariums, is situated between the two wings. It is on the same level as Phinney Avenue.

The unobstructed view of Puget Sound and the Olympic Mountains to the west and beautiful Woodland Park to the east makes this site one of the finest that could be desired.

NORSE HOME   SEATTLE, WASHINGTON   EDWARD KRISTIAN MAHLUM, AIA ARCHITECT

ENTRANCE LOBBY

The entrance lobby has glass walls toward the street and the Roof Promenade. Both the morning and afternoon sun will make this a cheerful center. Here visitors will lounge while waiting to see their friends and relatives in the Norse Home. Off the entrance lobby are the offices, cloakroom and elevator.

The Lobby opens onto the spacious Roof Promenade to the west which, with its gorgeous view, will provide an additional attraction for both members and their guests.

ENTRANCE LOBBY
NORSE HOME   SEATTLE, WASHINGTON.   EDWARD KRISTIAN MAHLUM A.I.A ARCHITECT

5-26-57

DREAM COME TRUE: Hearty handshakes and turning over the keys marked yesterday's dedication of the long-planned Norse Home at 5311 Phinney Av. From left, Frode Frodesen, vice chairman of the board of directors; Thor Bjornstad, building - committee chairman; Edward Mahlum, architect; Mrs. Mary Cleverley, representing the Federal Housing Administration and Paul P. Berg, chairman of the board of directors. Mrs. Cleverley will present a gold key to President Eisenhower. The F. H. A. is guaranteeing the $850,000 loan for the structure.

News clipping from 1957 with the exchange of the Gold Keys.

Original "infirmary" Nurses Station.

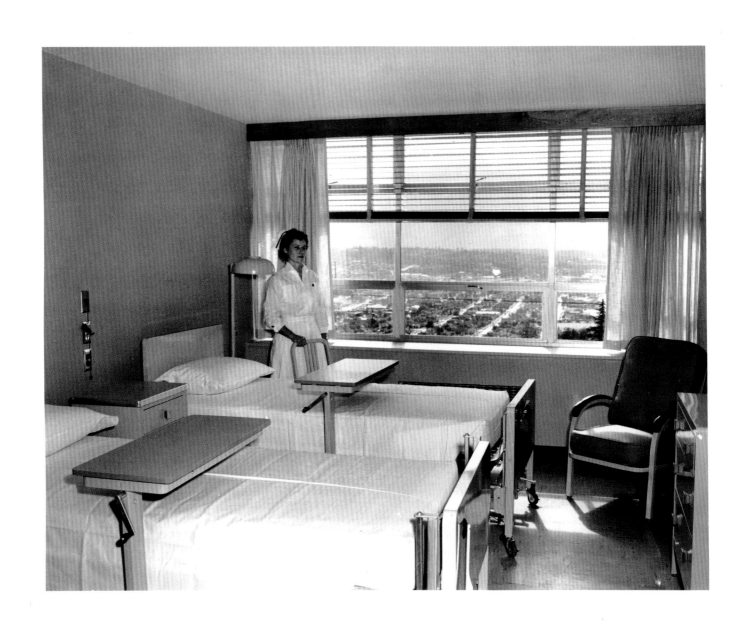

Original resident rooms for care on the infirmary floor.

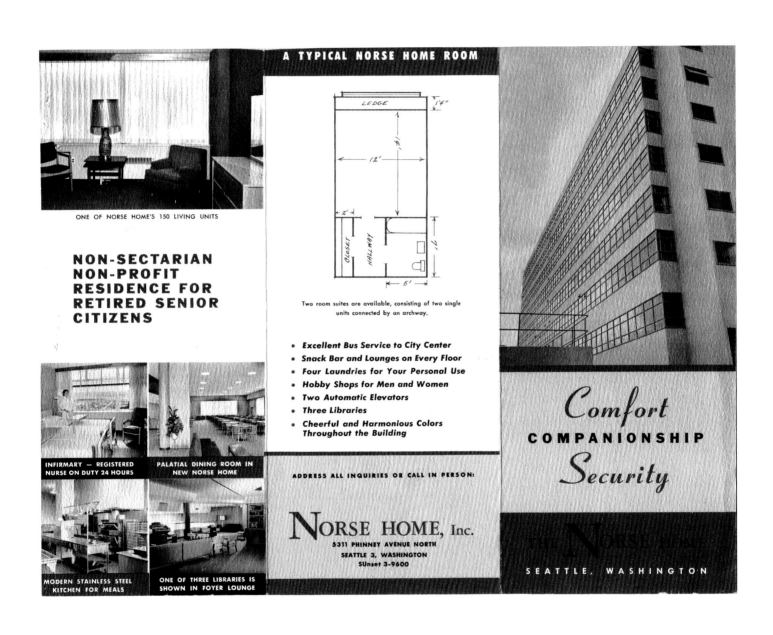

A TYPICAL NORSE HOME ROOM

LEDGE

1'4"

7'

12'

2'

CLOSET   HALLWAY

7'

5'

Two room suites are available, consisting of two single
units connected by an archway.

- *Excellent Bus Service to City Center*
- *Snack Bar and Lounges on Every Floor*
- *Four Laundries for Your Personal Use*
- *Hobby Shops for Men and Women*
- *Two Automatic Elevators*
- *Three Libraries*
- *Cheerful and Harmonious Colors Throughout the Building*

ONE OF NORSE HOME'S 150 LIVING UNITS

**NON-SECTARIAN
NON-PROFIT
RESIDENCE FOR
RETIRED SENIOR
CITIZENS**

INFIRMARY — REGISTERED
NURSE ON DUTY 24 HOURS

PALATIAL DINING ROOM IN
NEW NORSE HOME

MODERN STAINLESS STEEL
KITCHEN FOR MEALS

ONE OF THREE LIBRARIES IS
SHOWN IN FOYER LOUNGE

ADDRESS ALL INQUIRIES OR CALL IN PERSON:

NORSE HOME, Inc.
5311 PHINNEY AVENUE NORTH
SEATTLE 3, WASHINGTON
SUnset 3-9600

Comfort
COMPANIONSHIP
Security

THE NORSE HOME

SEATTLE, WASHINGTON

Pages 121-122: Two-sided hand out brochure showing room diagram and descriptions.

OPENED JUNE 16, 1957 • EDWARD MAHLUM, ARCHITECT, A.I.A.

VIEW OF THE NORSE HOME FROM THE EAST SIDE

THE NORSE HOME

**NON-SECTARIAN, NON-PROFIT
RESIDENCE FOR RETIRED
SENIOR CITIZENS**

The Norse Home, a comfortable residence for retired senior citizens, was the far-reaching goal of a few pioneer Norwegian-Americans.

The modern 6-story Norse Home, built of reinforced concrete, is the first of its kind to receive assistance from the Federal Housing Administration.

Rooms on the west side command a view of the majestic Olympic Mountains and Puget Sound. Rooms on the east side overlook Mount Baker, Woodland Park, and the Cascade Mountains.

The Norse Home, Inc., is a non-profit, non-sectarian residence built for senior citizens 60 years of age and over.

The affairs of the Norse Home are governed by a board of trustees. Board members are professional men and women of highest integrity, ability and experience.

"Just across the street from
BEAUTIFUL WOODLAND PARK"

Information ABOUT THE NORSE HOME

1. How is it financed?

Individuals, corporations, Norwegian Lodges, guilds, clubs and organizations donated and otherwise provided about $450,000 before construction commenced. Founders Fees and the FHA insured mortgage provided the balance of the building costs.

A substantial number of future residents of the Home will provide a portion of the funds required to repay the mortgage loan by paying Founders Fees priced at approximately one half of the over-all, average cost per unit. For this they are guaranteed their own living unit reserved for life.

2. How may I become a resident?

Those desiring to live at Norse Home must file a regular application which includes a financial statement. A health report is also required. Applications are considered by the board of directors.

Those fortunate enough to be accepted and coming in soon, pay Founders Fees priced at $7,000 for corner rooms or $6,000 for other rooms which includes $500 earnest money. The $500 earnest money must be paid when signing the contract and the balance when room is ready for occupancy.

3. May I change my mind?

An applicant, if accepted, may cancel his contract if this is done prior to moving to Norse Home, or even during the first three months of residence. If cancelled within this period, all but the earnest money will be returned when the living unit concerned has been disposed of.

4. What is the monthly charge at present and what does it cover?

The present charge of $~~107~~ 128,00 per month per person was originally established on the cost of living basis. Rates are computed upon actual costs and may be increased or decreased with changes in cost of living. 238,00

Two persons in one room pay $~~212~~ per month. One person in a two-room suite pays $~~142~~ per month. 155,00

The monthly charge covers food, heat, lights, laundry (other than personal), periodical maid service, temporary infirmary care, and many other items that make life at Norse Home rich and worthwhile.

5. What are the advantages of purchasing a unit at THE NORSE HOME?

You will enjoy lifetime use of your unit at a price very much less than the actual cost and have the privilege of living in comfortable surroundings, among congenial people in a modern, fireproof building. You will feel more secure with a registered nurse on duty at all times and with the infirmary available if you should become ill.

6. How do I get on the waiting list?

A person may get on the Waiting List by making regular application, together with health report, and after application is approved by paying $525. All but $25 of this is returnable if the applicant does not move into the Norse Home. The $500 applies on the regular Founders Fee. No interest is paid on this deposit, the loss of interest being the price the applicant pays for seniority on the Waiting List. It is advisable to make application from three to five years before expecting to move to Norse Home.

7. Infirmary charges for residents?

There is no charge for the first five days of each separate illness. After five days, the rate will be $2 per day in addition to the regular monthly rate.

A resident has the right to retain his room as long as he lives. However, in case of prolonged illness, the resident may have his furniture, etc., moved away or to one of the locked storage rooms, permitting occupancy of the living unit by another person. By so doing, the infirmary charge would be the same as the regular monthly charge.

8. Who will pay my doctor?

You choose your own doctor and pay his fee.

9. May I have a television?

Yes, you may bring your TV and a small charge of $5 per year will be made.

10. May I have a telephone?

There will be a telephone in each room and hotel-type service provided.

The regular monthly charge is included in the quoted monthly rates.

11. May I have my own furniture?

Wall-to-wall carpets and draperies are provided for each room. Residents may bring their own furniture and personal possessions, thus making the living unit truly "home."

12. What about parking?

Limited parking space is available at $5 per month.

13. What activities are available?

Hobby shops, games and social activities are available.

14. Will there be church services?

Yes, delivered by Pastors of all faiths.

15. May I have guests?

Residents are free to have guests and visitors at any reasonable time.

16. May I come and go as I please?

Residents are free to come and go as they choose. For periods of absence from 7 days and not to exceed 8 weeks, $6 per week is deducted from monthly charge.

Board of Directors 1993, President Trygve Jorgensen front row, second from right

Board of Directors 2000, President Trygve Kvalheim center front row.

Board of Directors 2011, Back row: John Rockom, Dagfinn Melby, President Konrad S. Uri, Robert Johnston. Front row: Executive Director Jennifer Jorgensen, Gunbjorg Gladstein, Carol Lindgren, Andrea Torland, and Sylvia Pugh.

1943 Solveig Guild.

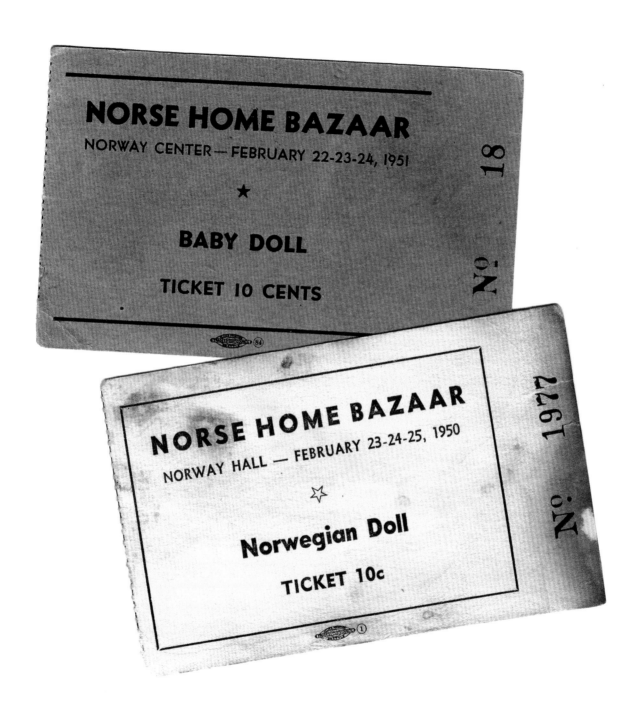

1950 and 1951 NORSE HOME Bazaar Raffle tickets (the actual tickets showing event and 10 c each).

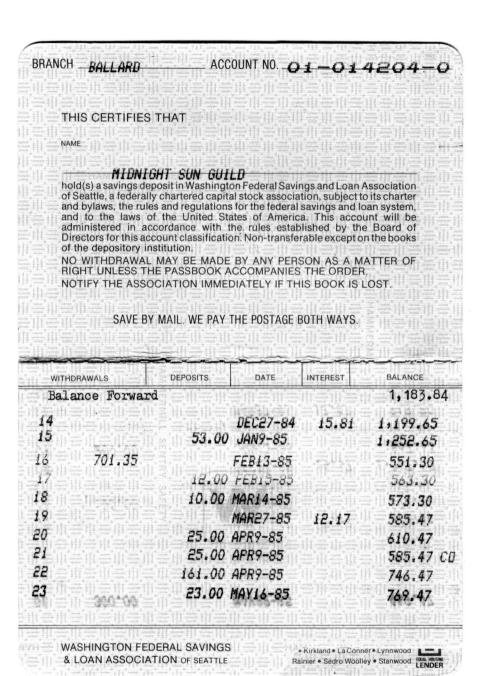

WITHDRAWALS	DEPOSITS	DATE	INTEREST	BALANCE
Balance Forward				1,183.84
14		DEC27-84	15.81	1,199.65
15	53.00	JAN9-85		1,252.65
16 701.35		FEB13-85		551.30
17	12.00	FEB13-85		563.30
18	10.00	MAR14-85		573.30
19		MAR27-85	12.17	585.47
20	25.00	APR9-85		610.47
21	25.00	APR9-85		585.47 CO
22	161.00	APR9-85		746.47
23	23.00	MAY16-85		769.47

Midnatsol Guild savings book from 1984.

Midnatsol Guild—40 Years of Service

A beautiful Silver Tea celebrating forty years of dedication to Norse Home was held in the Social Hall on April 10, 1984.

In June 1944 Klara Tynes invited twelve ladies to a beautiful luncheon and this was the beginning of Midnatsol Guild. The ladies were inspired by Inga Frodsen who spoke on the need for a home for retired Senior Citizens with all the comforts of life, including health care.

Though busy raising families, these twelve found time and energy for dinners, dances at the old Norway Hall, luncheons, cookie sales, garden sales and other fund-raising activities.

Four charter members, Klara Tynes, Emma Birkvold, Jenny Oakvik and Signy Floathe (along with twenty-eight others) continue to work for Norse Home today.

Midnatsol meets the second Tuesday of each month. The group's goal is to raise money for the Health Center.

Highlights of the Midnatsol year are a 17th of May Celebration in the Health Center when the ladies, dressed in their Norwegian costumes, come with a cake and all the trimmings to provide a special program. October is the annual fund-raising luncheon. In December they have a Christmas Party for patients of the Health Center and each one receives a decorated cannister of homemade cookies to have in his or her room. Their last meeting in May is a special dinner meeting for the guild members in a good restaurant.

Norse Home congratulates and thanks the membership for caring and sharing.

Midnatsol Guild article celebrates 40 years (1944-1984).

THE U.S. FLAG FLYING ON THE POLE IN THE YARD OF THE NORSE HOME WAS FLOWN OVER THE CAPITOL OF THE UNITED STATES ON AUGUST 27, 1981 AT THE REQUEST OF U.S. SEN. HENRY M. JACKSON

NORSE HOME ARCHITECT EDWARD MAHLUM LISTENS AS SENATOR HENRY M. ADDRESSES ASSEMBLED GUESTS AT THE FLAG RAISING CEREMONY, JUNE 6th

Senator Henry Jackson presenting a Flag to the NORSE HOME.

1985 Bake Sale, Winnie Peterson, center, NORSE HOME resident.

L. to r.: Jean Bennett, v.p. of Inga Frodesen Guild; Ruth Pearson, a past pres. and daughter of Haldis Jules, founder of the guild; Anne Marie Steiner, a past pres. and the daughter of Inga Frodesen; Joanne Varney, current pres. of the guild; and Sissel Peterson, long-time secretary.

1990 news clipping, picture of Inga Frodesen Guild's 30th anniversary.

1991 Woodlawn Guild 50th Anniversary.

Ticket sale at Norse Home Bazaar where members took turns at sales table. Pictured with display Lilly Bjornstad, resident at Norse Home and Solveig Berg, Femboringen president.

1993 Femboringen Guild, NORSE HOME Bazaar item Barbie Doll with hand made clothing by then Guild President Solveig Berg (now a NORSE HOME resident), and Lilly Bjornstad, guild member and former NORSE HOME resident.

Certificate
of
Appreciation

This certificate is presented to

The Femboringen Guild

in appreciation for the valuable contribution

given to *The Norse Home*.

Our sincere gratitude is extended to you this

22 day of *April* *1992*.

Signed *Maggie Riekerk*

1992 - The installing of the traffic light on Phinney Avenue and 53rd Street as a result of the Femboring Guild efforts.

2010 Volunteer greeters from the Valkyrien Lodge of the Daughters of Norway, Sissel Tangen and Kaaren Sterlington at the annual NORSE HOME *Julebord*.

A 2010 Smorgasbord volunteer, and former board member Bernice Chouery offering a raffle prize from the Nordmansforbunder organization.

2011 Seterjenten Guild prepares Potato Balls for the annual *Kumle* dinner in record breaking time, over 500 in 45 minutes. From left, Borghild Erickson, Myrtle Ryan, Torbjorg Solberg, Else Driflot, Toni Platou.

1995 Welcome sign for Queen Sonja in former lobby.

Photo/Greg Farrar

Norway's Queen Sonja smiles as she receives a bouquet of roses from Norse Home resident Lilly Bjornstad during the queen's tour. She is introduced by Norse Home Board Member Lise Berger, right, dressed in a traditional Norwegian costume.

1995 news clipping with the Queen being greeted by
NORSE HOME resident Lilly Bjornstad and board member Lise Berger.

SOME "MAD" MILLINERY BY THE WOMEN WHO DE-SIGNED IT: From left, THE MESDAMES BERIT LAR-SON, IN TOPPER MADE OF COLLANDER AND TRAY; MRS. LORA CLOCKSIN, A LAMPSHADE TRIMMED WITH LEMONS, AND MRS. CHARLOTTE WEHRN, A MARTIAN CREATION.

MRS. HELGA NANTHRUP, 88,

Senior citizens at Norse Home, retirement resi-dence, let their Thursday evening social "go right to their heads." The reason: It was a "Mad Hat-ter's Tea Party," with everyone modeling zany chapeaux of their own creation. Toppers were trimmed with kitchen utensils and Christmas-tree ornaments, lemons and lampshades. The refresh-ment committee even served hat-shaped cookies. —Times photos by Richard S. Heyza.

1962 – Silly Hat Day featured in local newspaper, an activity still held at NORSE HOME, usually in the month of January.

1997 – Residents enjoying one of many dance events.

October 2002 – Administrator Robert Solem (right) and Social Worker Judy Rosman (left), greeting each other and residents in the lobby.

2002 – Residents are always a big help in getting the NORSE HOME newsletter in the mail.

Priceless views from every NORSE HOME apartment.

2010 Resident Elise Shogren as Minnie Mouse in one of the annual Readers Theater peformances. In 2012 Elsie turned 102 and has performed in 19 consecutive years of Readers Theater.

July 2010 – Molly Holscher, the author and director of all the famous NORSE HOME Readers Theater productions performed by NORSE HOME resdients.

2011 – Resident Emma Vatn (who as a young adult was at the NORSE HOME ground breaking) enjoys having coffee in the NORSE HOME bistro with a guest.

2011 – Social meet and greet before annual Potato Ball dinner includes author Junius Rochester on the left and Board President Konrad S. Uri in the center.

2011 – *Julebord* Fundraiser and Smorgasbord Dinner.

2012 – Lucille Hayes feeding the fish in the main Garden courtyard.

2011 – Jennifer Jorgensen greeting guest and resident Ingvald Jensen.

2011 – Norse Home front sign.

2012 – The NORSE HOME building as it is today. From Phinney Avenue North.

2012 – View of the NORSE HOME from Ballard.

2012 – Ad for NORSE HOME.

(continued from page 96)

promised to deliver one of NORSE HOME's Gold Keys to President Dwight D. Eisenhower. The latter gesture had considerable meaning: President Eisenhower had supported the project, and NORSE HOME was the first FHA loan designed to help elder citizens find reasonably priced, comfortable housing. That summer a letter from President Dwight D. Eisenhower arrived thanking the Board for his NORSE HOME Gold Key.

LARGE SUMS

Cost of building and furnishing the NORSE HOME was estimated by August Buschmann in 1950 at "about $550,000." In 1955, an estimate was given (perhaps without furnishings) of $418,333. Later estimates grew to over $700,000 with continued fundraising efforts and help from the Federal Housing Administration (below). One estimate exceeded $1,000,000.

How were funds raised? The answer is — except for controversial investments in two oil companies (which were arranged by August Buschmann and paid handsome dividends) and a professional fundraising drive — monies were acquired the old-fashioned way. That is: Guild activities and The Norwegian Hospital Association relentlessly staged projects and events; generous Lodge donations were received; personal solicitation by Board members and others (e.g., August Buschmann was responsible for approximately $70,400 in private donations); special dinners, teas, bazaars and the raffle of a Cadillac car donated by August Buschmann ($14,000) were helpful.

John Mahlum accompanied his father, Ed Mahlum, architect of NORSE HOME, on several fundraising treks. In the 1950s, John recalls standing on Market Street as a young boy with his father and several others selling "bonds" for NORSE HOME. John did this several times and it made a lasting impression. The scene would be indelible to a young mind: his father and other gentlemen in suits and ties, waving printed material at passersby.

"Outside" players in this campaign were journalists like The Seattle Times' Byron Fish, who on February 16, 1956, used his column to extol "A Dream of more than 30 years." Fish wrote:

"… many Norwegian organizations are behind the campaign. The success of Norway Center, opened five years ago, gives them all good reason for optimism."

Fish also observed that the Washington State Health Department called NORSE HOME… "the most modern and best planned of any seen to date." He affirmed that although NORSE HOME is the dream of Norwegian immigrants, its facilities are "non-sectarian and open to other nationalities."

DOCUMENTS AND PERMITS

Dr. T.W. Buschmann's downtown Seattle office in the Stimson Building served as the campaign headquarters for NORSE HOME. Buschmann's private secretary kept NORSE HOME books, at no cost to the campaign. Office space was made available for meetings. All campaign correspondence was accomplished at this location, including sending notices far and wide. Banking and other financial transactions were also done in the Buschmann offices. Upon retaining Edward K. Mahlum as architect for the planned NORSE HOME, several permits and related construction tasks were achieved at the Stimson Building address.

An example of Dr. Buschmann's professional office services and his active involvement in the design and construction of NORSE HOME occurred on June 25, 1951. In writing to John B. Cain, Superintendent of Buildings, City of Seattle, on NORSE HOME stationery, Dr. Buschmann agreed to the following "reservations" regarding the home's preliminary architectural drawings:

1. The entire area of the property (Block 72, Supplemental Woodland Park Addition) must remain in one unit at all times.
2. The surgery and other areas of the Infirmary must be used for and in connection with the care of bona fide inmates of the NORSE HOME only.
3. The garage must be used for ambulances, undertakers and official personnel connected with the NORSE HOME only.
4. The Assembly-Dining Room, when used as an assembly room, must be for affairs in

connection with activities for NORSE HOME residents only.

5. The Recreation-Lounge will remain permanently furnished as per plans only, and it must never be used for added assembly hall seating.

6. The roof promenade must have a sign posted under glass stating that its maximum capacity at any time is 25 persons. This sign must be posted at or near the emergency exit.

7. It is further agreed that the requirements of this letter will be placed on our records and that all future operating managements, owners, or lessees of the building will be informed of the above agreements and conditions.

LOOKING GOOD

Before moving ahead, a list of recommendations was prepared regarding appearance and utilitarian aspects of NORSE HOME. To see matters clearly and professionally, other retirement homes had been studied by the Committee, including Martha and Mary in Poulsbo, Washington.

This "wish list" included matters such as:

1. The building taking advantage of the entire plat of land (no sprawling lawns or gardens);
2. admitting sunlight wherever possible;
3. solaria;
4. alcoves on each side of the halls, but not facing each other;
5. use of ramps instead of stairways;
6. two elevators large enough to hold stretchers;
7. toilets, wash basins and possibly a bath installed between every two rooms;
8. closets equally distributed
9. an assembly room seating at least 200 persons;
10. a delivery entrance on the basement level where storerooms are located;

11. a clinic;

12. offices and other non-residential rooms located in areas with the least sunshine. Other facilities mentioned were a shop, museum (which did not happen) and library.

EDWARD KRISTIAN MAHLUM, A.I.A. (1909-1998)

Although born in Seattle, Edward K. Mahlum was taken by his Norwegian parents back to the Old Country for eighteen years. His studies in Norway included several languages and the basics of a high school curriculum. In 1928 he returned to America, entered North Dakota State University, emerging in 1934 with a degree in architecture.

Mahlum spent his youth in Lillehammer, Norway's winter sports center. He took advantage of his surroundings by becoming a champion speed skater, winning first prize in record time in a 500-meter event. He also played tennis and soccer. His early Norway years exposed him to what would become a lifelong love of music. Mahlum played the piano and valve trombone and participated in school and other bands. After graduating from North Dakota State College in Fargo, he joined hobos riding the rails to Seattle, Washington.

After working in an architecture firm in Minnesota, he returned to Seattle — his birthplace — in 1940. He was successfully established in his profession when the NORSE HOME project came into view in the 1940s-1950s. After interviews with several Seattle-based architects (at least seven, their bids dating to 1946), the NORSE HOME Board chose Mahlum. His Norwegian credentials may have brightened his prospects with the Board, but Mahlum's successful architectural practice was a more important factor.

There was more to the project than designing a facility for older citizens. Edward Mahlum and the Board chose a different path than existed at the time. Many retirement homes took all available funds from residents. The NORSE HOME Board recognized that older people, although willing to pay for good accommodations, wished to retain money for themselves. In other words, a kind of partnership was envisioned between the facility and its residents. To achieve this goal required insurance of NORSE HOME mortgages — a tall order at the time.

Ed Mahlum became part of the fabric of NORSE HOME. He put his ideas on paper, contacted people, helped raise funds, remained available as the years dragged on, and always believed that the Board would find ways to fund construction of a model retirement home. He also served for a period on the NORSE HOME Board.

An example of Mahlum's tenacity and interest is seen in a letter he wrote in 1956 to Sons of Norway Supreme President Gerhard N. Sonnesuyn, in which he stated:

> *"With the solid background and foundation already laid through the many years of successful lodge work by the thousands of members of Sons of Norway I think that we as a group are ready and able to make a still greater contribution to the growth of our country by collectively shouldering a greater share of the burdens and obligations of citizenship... Let us double our membership by doing a good deed for the old. With 75,000 members, an assessment of $10.00 each is $750,000, which means that we, by pulling together, could build a first class retirement home every other year for a yearly assessment of $10.00."*

In 1962, the year of the Seattle World's Fair, Edward K. Mahlum received the St. Olav's Medal for his help in achieving Norway's liberation from the wartime occupation.

IMAGES OF NORSE HOME

The first graphic representations of a retirement home on Phinney Ridge showed large buildings with towers and wings in several directions. One sample sketch resembled a Swiss-like chateau. Another version had a large cupola and the hint of a small "widow's walk" on the peaked roof. Wings, alcoves and gardens were depicted. Early sketches in ads for NORSE HOME described the building as having "Scandinavian design, built of brick and stone."

However, the eventual NORSE HOME was Edward K. Mahlum's gracious rectangular structure, stretching between North 53rd and North 54th Streets. It contains all the suggested amenities and proper spaces for efficient management by the staff and fully provides for the comfort and ease of residents.

THE FEDERAL HOUSING ADMINISTRATION

With the NORSE HOME'S backing, architect Edward K. Mahlum stretched his talents. He contacted several friends with Norwegian backgrounds: U.S. Senators Henry M. Jackson and Warren G. Magnuson, and Washington State Governor Arthur B. Langlie. They agreed with Mahlum that more could be done. The Federal Housing Administration (FHA) offered financing to young couples for housing needs. Mahlum thought that the federal agency might look at new opportunities. He met with FHA officials to convince them that a special fund should be used to aid housing built by non-profit corporations exclusively for the aged. President Dwight D. Eisenhower agreed. The FHA kitty held $20,000,000 and NORSE HOME would get its share.

The next step was to convince Congress to pass legislation confirming the new use of FHA housing funds (for elderly citizens). With the aid of home state U.S. Senators and members of the House of Representatives, a bill was introduced allowing non-profit organizations to qualify for FHA insurance of mortgages on residences for the aged.

After eight years of design work and negotiations, Mahlum's professionalism and tenacity, and the dedication of the Board and its friends in high places, resulted in "their" bill passing Congress in June 1956. The NORSE HOME project was the first such FHA project in the nation.

On February 24, 1958, the Federal National Mortgage Association sent a check for $103,863.79 to NORSE HOME, noting that it represented "the maximum amount we can pay during the first year toward the deduction of the... $700,000 loan." The Dream was almost a reality.

Ed Mahlum received a letter from B. Thor Bjornstad, Chairman of the NORSE HOME Building Committee, in mid-October 1957. The letter's second paragraph is quoted in full:

"However, it is not only for the efficient performance of your duties as Architect that we are grateful. Your willingness to help us in matters outside the scope of the contract has also been greatly appreciated. The numerous tasks which you have cheerfully performed in the interest of the Home, whether or not they were related to Architecture, have been of great help to us over the last several years and if it was in my power to do, I would recommend you as recipient of a medal for extraordinary service performed above and beyond the normal call of duty."

THE "FOUNDERS" OF NORSE HOME

Before final details were settled, the FHA asked for a listing of "supporting organizations" favoring the NORSE HOME. Here is the response, prepared by Ole J. Andreassen, member of the Board of Directors:

LEIF ERIKSON LODGE No. 1, Sons of Norway, Seattle, Washington
KNUTE ROCKNE LODGE No. 12, Sons of Norway, Seattle, Washington
VALKYRIEN LODGE No. 1, Daughters of Norway, Seattle, Washington
NORWEGIAN MALE CHORUS, Seattle, Washington

(A note was inserted here stating that Leif Erikson Lodge No. 1, Knute Rockne Lodge, Valkyrien Lodge No. 1, and Norwegian Male Chorus are the owners of NORWAY CENTER in Seattle, a building which was erected in 1951, costing $500,000, and "is operating very successfully.")

TERJE VIKEN LODGE No. 31, Sons of Norway, Seattle, Washington
BREIDABLIK LODGE No. 10, Sons of Norway, Seattle, Washington
NORWEGIAN COMMERCIAL CLUB, Seattle, Washington
NORWEGIAN LADIES CHORUS, Seattle, Washington

NORDLANDSLAGET, INC., Seattle, Washington
OSLO LODGE No. 35, Daughters of Norway, Bremerton, Washington
LYNGBLOMSTEN LODGE No. 27, Daughters of Norway, Aberdeen, Washington

Mr. Andreassen then mentions "outright donations" and support of bazaars, musical and other affairs from the above organizations. He also notes that nineteen GUILDS, with average memberships of twenty individuals, are "dedicated to furnish individual rooms, lounges and other facilities in the NORSE HOME."

OPPOSITION

For the record, one Sons of Norway lodge withheld financial support, while supporting the idea of a retirement home for elder Norwegian citizens. Alfred K. Ostness, President of Sons of Norway, District Lodge No. 2, Spokane, Washington, appeared to be influenced by the Supreme Lodge, Sons of Norway, in Minneapolis, Minnesota. Mr. E.B. Hauke, President of the Supreme Lodge, thought that because the Supreme Lodge was, among other things, an insurance company, certain laws might prevent them from loaning money to NORSE HOME.

August Buschmann's correspondence with both Mr. Hauke and Mr. Ostness also suggests that the Spokane lodge felt closer to a Coeur d'Alene home than a projected similar institution in Seattle. There was more to the story: Mr. Ostness was apparently dismayed, as were many of the lodge's members (the Tordenskjold Guild was mentioned), that NORSE HOME "would be open to all people." Mr. Buschmann replied to Mr. Ostness in this manner:"… bear in mind that the Sons and Daughters of Norway will always control the operation of this Home, and consequently, I believe the greatest percentage or at least the majority of the members will be lodge members of at least Norwegians or Scandinavians."

PETER D. WICK (1892-1988)

Peter D. Wick, Sr. was one of nine children born on his family's farm in Syvde, Norway. In 1913, he emigrated to America. At first he and a partner built apartments during the war. During the 1930s, he became superintendent of construction for the Olympic Hot Springs pool on the Olympic Peninsula. In 1951, he and his son Andrew P. Wick founded Wick Construction Company in Seattle.   In Seattle and elsewhere Wick Construction Company gained a reputation for reliable, timely work, including the Hearthstone, the Sheraton Hotel in Spokane, and various special facilities at the 1962 Seattle World's Fair. King Olaf V of Norway awarded Peter D. Wick the St. Olaf medal in 1962. After a bidding process, Wick was chosen by the NORSE HOME Board to work with architect Ed Mahlum.

The 1956 enabling legislation passed by Congress to allow FHA mortgage insurance for elder citizen housing gave a green light to Wick Construction Company of Seattle. Wick immediately moved ahead on its contract with NORSE HOME. At first, funds were available to construct only three floors of the proposed seven-story structure. Because of Peter Wick's belief in the Board's resolve, and Edward Mahlum's talents and work, two additional floors were added to the building by Wick.

Peter Wick was among those who hailed the new FHA rules passed by Congress for an FHA mortgage insurance program for NORSE HOME and for non-profit retirement facilities throughout the country.

In September 1957, the NORSE HOME Building Committee wrote Peter D. Wick, expressing appreciation for his "personal interest in this project" and his "daily inspiring visits to the job (and) allowing us additional time on monthly payments when we encountered financial difficulties."

Supporting contractors, besides Wick Construction, were low bidders Ballard Plumbing & Heating (mechanical) and Beckstrom Electric (electrical work).

AUGUST BUSCHMANN'S TESTIMONY

Responding to questions from O.L. Ejde of the Norwegian Language newspaper *Washington-Posten* in June 1966, August Buschmann described why he gave time and money to help finance NORSE HOME:

"I came from Norway with my parents over sixty-five years ago, landing in Tacoma, on June 7, 1891. Father had met with reverses before leaving Norway and decided that America offered a better future...

My brother (Trygve W. Buschmann) and I earned our first money selling newspapers, The Tacoma News, on the streets of Tacoma...

The older I get, the more I appreciate what it means to be a citizen of the United States of America and permitted to live here where we can all enjoy our precious free enterprise system and also share our many advantages with those who are not citizens...

Some years ago I tried to provide fairly comfortable living quarters for several elderly people who were deserving but had little money. . . I commenced to realize how difficult it was to find, at a reasonable price, comfortable quarters in pleasant surroundings, with congenial people, for these elderly folks...

I consider it a privilege to donate time and money to this project (NORSE HOME), and exercising this privilege helps discharge one of our most sacred and necessary duties which should not in any way be considered an imposition or a burden."

WATCHING FROM A DISTANCE

ANNA and HARALD LARSSEN and their children, Mari and Halvor, often visited ANNA's precious Woodland Park. They usually parked their car on Phinney Avenue near the water tower, the highest point of the hill.

In the mid 1950s, a nearby hole in the ground slowly grew into the NORSE HOME. The LARSSEN family watched this imposing building emerge, floor by floor. Eventually, HARALD's friends invited him to help with wood-working projects: moldings, doorways, panels, cabinets. These instances brought him in close touch with Peter D. Wick, NORSE HOME General Contractor and also a Norwegian. The halls, stairways and rooms of NORSE HOME became familiar to HARALD. He occasionally brought his kids to watch him work on what he viewed as a Norwegian monument.

On May 26, 1957, HARALD, ANNA and their children stood as spectators at the back of a group of dignitaries to watch contractor Peter D. Wick ceremoniously open the NORSE HOME with a GOLD KEY. After almost 30 years of struggle, a new building and a new era had begun.

Chapter IV. Making It Happen

"IT CAN BE DONE"

"WE CAN DO IT"

(A Challenge from NORSE HOME Advance Gift Committee Chairman,
August Buschmann)

Anna's Fourth Letter

Dear Ulrikka,

It has been too long since I wrote you about our American life. Harald is thinking of retiring but will continue to do small carpentry jobs. His ship-building profession has changed. And he admits to arthritis pains in his shoulders and back. Because everything he does at the ship company is very physical, he knows that he cannot work forever. My situation is different. I've been a Charge Nurse on a floor at Ballard General Hospital for the past eight years. Although my days can stretch to ten hours, and I'm on my feet a lot, most of my time is spent assigning patients to other nurses and problem-solving when necessary. For example, last week I had to help with a patient who had a dry cough, some choking, and at times could not breathe. After several ups and downs, she finally went to the Lord. Although these things happen, it's never easy and often complicated when members of the patient's family are nearby. Some weekends Harald and I drive north to the small town of Edison. It has a small Norwegian community, several churches and restaurants, and sits next to both a salt water bay called Samish and a slough, which is a small, slow-moving river. The countryside is flat and we find places that sell seafood, vegetables and cheeses. A few miles away are some of the largest and most beautiful tulip farms in the world. Harald and I call these weekend trips "little honeymoons." Although the kids also know this country, Halvor and Mari are on their own. They are both in school and Halvor is working weekends at a restaurant. Don't forget us, Ulrikka. We miss you all.

Anna

Harald's Fourth Letter

Thorvald,

You are a faithful correspondent. Every year I receive several letters from you. Although we both left Norway many years ago, our memories of Haugesund and our trips into the mountains remain clear. I'm pleased that you and your family have found a good life in Wisconsin. We have been equally lucky in the state of Washington. My career is changing - too much physical effort - but our children and the busy city of Seattle keep everything moving. Both Mari and Halvor are wonderful skiers. They prefer downhill rather than our favorite cross-country, but the mountains in this part of the world have many attractions, including comfortable resorts and lodges. Anna and I take short trips around this beautiful country. We also are active in several Norwegian organizations, including the Sons of Norway. Our neighborhood is home to many Scandinavians and the May 17th celebration means a noisy parade down the main street. Our community of Ballard is home to many young couples so the area is busy with coffee shops, restaurants and bars. Music is everywhere. For a peaceful time we visit Woodland Park and its large zoo. Anna has particularly fond memories of this green area. She came here as a young girl and couldn't speak a word of English. We'll show you all these places if I you come to the Pacific Northwest. When you first see the Pacific Northwest it will seem like Norway. Everyone sends love to your family.

Harald

Underway

Fitting Everything Together

NORSE HOME's life since its gala opening in 1957 traces an arc of changes, renovations, celebrations, staffing evolvement and Volunteer auxiliary and Guild activities. The presence of NORSE HOME on Phinney Ridge looms for everyone connected with the project — and for many passersby.

THE 1950s: PAUL P. BERG; FOUNDER'S FEE PLAN; MEMORIAL FUND

PAUL P. BERG (1910-1992)

Paul Peterson Berg was President of the Leif Erikson Lodge four times. From that vantage point he was involved directly in early efforts to plan and build NORSE HOME. In 1955, he was elected president of the NORSE HOME Board of Trustees, and served during the building years until 1965. Paul was awarded the St. Olaf Medal by the late King Olaf of Norway at the 1962 Seattle World's Fair. He was married to Marion Carol Jenseth.

The years of Paul Berg's NORSE HOME presidency were crucial. The Campaign to raise funds was underway. However, many NORSE HOME supporters were losing heart. Finding resources proved to be an arduous job. Under Berg's guidance, NORSE HOME successfully completed the Campaign and a number of milestones were reached; Architect Edward K. Mahlum came aboard; a Federal Housing Administration change in rules occurred (with the help of many) allowing NORSE HOME to receive a federally guaranteed loan; a dedication ceremony took place; and on May 26, 1957, the front door of NORSE HOME was opened by General Contractor P.D. Wick with a GOLD KEY.

FOUNDER'S FEE PLAN

Upon its opening, a Founder's Fee Plan was in place to regularize the cost of entering NORSE HOME and to help applicants who could not afford the residence. The first Founder's Fee was $5,500. Monthly charge for food and services was set at $90. When the fees were established, the unit cost was lowered beyond the recommended amount "to enable as many as possible to take advantage of the services at NORSE HOME." For bookkeeping and tax purposes, Founder's Fees were dropped under the administration of Robert Solem in the late 1990s.

In fact, NORSE HOME gave forty-four rooms to Norwegians who were unable to pay the Founder's Fee. One applicant insisted that he should have a free room because he had made a donation during the fundraising campaign. He was politely refused. His donation had been five dollars.

MEMORIAL FUND

Because NORSE HOME had been established to welcome residents from every income level, it became clear that in a few instances the ability of a few to meet minimum costs was in question. Board member Ole Andreassen, upon learning that so-called "welfare" cases could enter NORSE HOME if modest amounts of money were found to supplement the balance of their bill, suggested a Memorial Fund. At the February 17, 1959, Board meeting, C.K. Anderson made a motion that a Memorial Fund be set up to assist those who could not otherwise enter NORSE HOME. It was further suggested that the Guilds be asked to support the new fund, which they agreed to do.

Board minutes remind readers, as well as staff and residents, that NORSE HOME's mission includes helping people in diverse ways. An example: When a question arose about the difficulty a NORSE HOME couple was having in paying Health Center costs, Board member Don Thoreson stated that "part of our mission… includes a certain amount of charity."

(It was in the 1980s that a NORSE HOME Endowment Fund would be realized, which also assisted residents with limited incomes and in times of emergency. Today this fund is known as Resident's Assistance Fund.)

THE 1960s: A NEW GUILD; A CROSSWALK; A BUS SHELTER; CROWN PRINCE HARALD

In January 1960, the Inga Frodesen Guild was formed to honor Mrs. Frodesen, the "mother" of NORSE HOME. The Frodesen family expressed their thanks and pleasure. The founder was Mrs. Sverre Jules, who assumed the role as first president of the new Guild. (Inga Frodesen had been ill for some time. She died on April 14, 1963.)

After a few "near misses," August Buschmann announced that the city had agreed to place a crosswalk near the entrance to NORSE HOME. Despite the new pedestrian crossing, a resident was hit by a truck while walking in the new crosswalk in November 1961. A happy ending: In September 1992, City Councilman George Benson arranged a traffic light at the nervous crosswalk.

With the cooperation of Metro, the regional transportation organization, a cozy bus shelter was installed near the main entrance. Colorful murals inside the shelter were created by residents of NORSE HOME and Columbia Lutheran Home.

Also during the 1960s, NORSE HOME staff developed a series of local day trips and visits. The trips proved successful and have been scheduled ever since.

Crown Prince Harald of Norway visited NORSE HOME on January 13, 1964, a memorable event for residents.

A sad note: August Buschmann, principal fundraiser and loyal supporter of NORSE HOME during its early days, died in 1964.

Not long after NORSE HOME's doors were opened with the GOLD KEY, George C. Olsen sat down at NORSE HOME's grand piano. He played, while his wife and children picked up other instruments. Together they sang and performed a roll call of old-time tunes. The Olsen family inadvertently initiated a long and appreciated tradition of musical entertainment in the dining hall. Members of the Buschmann family continue the tradition at Christmas by playing the harp.

THE 1970s: SECURITY; MANAGING AN ASSET; QUIRKS AND MILESTONES

NORSE HOME security is never far from the minds of staff members, residents and the Board. With an eye to the vulnerability of a facility for seniors, a night watchman was hired in September 1972. Today NORSE HOME has 24-hour security managed by the Building Services Department.

Only nine years after the death of his brother August, a eulogy was delivered at the February 20, 1973 Board meeting in recognition of the death of Dr. Trygve W. Buschmann, longtime past president of NORSE HOME. Members of the Board stood in a moment of silence to honor Dr. Buschmann. A month later, the Board was informed that Dr. Buschmann had bequeathed $5,000 to NORSE HOME.

Periodically, NORSE HOME has compared its services and fees to similar facilities in Greater Seattle. Among other facilities examined in the late 1970s: Bayview Manor; Exeter House; Horizon House; Hearthstone; Judson Park; Kenney Home; Parkshore; Wesley Gardens; Northwest Danish Home. After examining these surveys, NORSE HOME's services and fees were found to be competitive or better. (A survey by the Witz Co. in 2010 came to the same conclusion.)

A great day! In March 1979, NORSE HOME's FHA mortgage was paid in full with a balloon payment — seven years before it was due.

Among the many ways to raise funds, family entertainment is popular and successful. NORSE HOME, with Anne Marie Frodesen Steiner at the helm, made arrangements to show the film "Northern Lights" at Ballard's Bay Theater on April 26, 1979. That evening was billed as a private showing, one day before the film opened to the public. The event was advertised as a Benefit Performance for NORSE HOME. In brief, the film depicted the Nonpartisan League in North Dakota during the early 1900s, and described lives of Norwegians and Swedes who participated in that political movement.

A milestone occurred on October 30, 1979, when, for the first time, the top three Board officer positions were held by women: Peggy Stjern, President; Anne Marie Frodesen Steiner, Vice-President; Emma Varney, Secretary.

THE 1980s: TWENTY-FIFTH ANNIVERSARY; MAJOR CHANGES, ESPECIALLY IN THE PHYSICAL PLANT; A RESIDENT'S COUNCIL; NEW POLICIES AND SERVICES.

THE TWENTY-FIFTH ANNIVERSARY

ANNA and HARALD LARSSEN joined a NORSE HOME Champagne dinner, with restaurateur Ivar Haglund serving as Honorary Campaign Chairman. The main event at the June 5, 1982, celebration was to toast NORSE HOME's Twenty-Fifth Anniversary.

NORSE HOME Trustees called the party the kickoff to a "Campaign,"because $1.5 million was sought for building improvements. The entire community was invited to the open house celebration, and 174 attended. Chairman Haglund pulled winning numbers from 5,000 tickets sold. First prize was a SAS round trip to Norway for two. Net proceeds from the raffle totaled over $5,000. ANNA and HARALD didn't win any big prizes, but they returned home with two paintings by a Norwegian artist. ANNA also learned more about the professional nursing and general health care at NORSE HOME.

The final event of the Twenty-Fifth celebration was a Silent Auction at 6:30 P.M. on June 29. Hors d'oeuvres and no-host wines were served. Auction items included sterling silver spoons, an oil seascape painting by Professor August Werner, a hand-knitted sweater and afghan, crystal decanters and restaurant dinners. Collector's items were also available, including a family Bible from 1889, illustrated by Gustave Doré; a radio-phonograph from the 1930s; and a Hammond electric organ.

MAJOR STEPS

After the Twenty-Fifth birthday celebration, and after residents and staff had experienced a "breaking-in" period, it was clear that several large features should be added to NORSE HOME. Bids were let for those projects. Among the winning contractors was architect John Mahlum, son of NORSE HOME's original architect, Ed Mahlum. Following are examples of those significant projects.

PHYSICAL PLANT

All physical properties must, in time, suffer wear. NORSE HOME, a busy, successful community, was faced with the expenses and inconvenience of renovation. Funds for a Capital Campaign were discussed. Ed Mahlum, designer of NORSE HOME, brought his fellow architect and son, John Mahlum, and partner, Vincent Norfors, to a Board meeting. The main topic was a survey of NORSE HOME's physical needs. A secondary topic was how to raise funds to accomplish the recommended tasks. Specific steps were proposed by the architectural firm of Mahlum, Mahlum, and Norfors, led by John Mahlum. Its overall proposal promised to: 1) assess the entire facility; 2) recommend general design solutions; 3) use consultants as needed. By September of 1980, the Mahlum recommendations were in hand. The Board undertook preparations for a Capital Improvements Campaign.

FUNDS TO PURCHASE

Among the first projects paid for by the Capital Improvements Campaign were the following: Install new drapes throughout the building; insulate windows; refurbish the Social Hall with new carpeting and Levelor shades; install window valances and vinyl wall covering; purchase chairs and tables; purchase a new Emergency Generator (see below); enlarge and modernize the Laundry.

By 1985, the following projects were funded by the Campaign:

- Roof repair and installation of new flashing

- Social Hall renovation

- New fluorescent lighting in the dining room

- Boilers were made more efficient

- Fire extinguishing system installed in the kitchen range hood

- Building exterior painted

- Laundry room renovated and upgraded

- Activity areas renovated and upgraded

- Reception area renovated and upgraded

EMERGENCY ELEVATOR

In 1983, an Emergency elevator was installed in NORSE HOME. Donated labor, material and money made this facility possible. Board members Art Lie, an electrical engineer, and Peter Knudsen drew plans and selected a location for the elevator. The professional hook-up was done by Lunde Electric. Lunde provided material at cost and labor at a reduced rate. Other helpers: Karl Larsen, with his truck; the Phil Varnes family gave a battery charger; the Trygve Bjornstads provided a generous financial contribution.

Another advantage of the elevator installation was that the accompanying sixty-kilowatt diesel generator can provide power in case of an emergency. If there was a power failure the generator could support essential lighting, one resident elevator, Health Center equipment, kitchen coffee makers, exhaust fans, and circulating pumps for heating.

THE VAN — ONE OF SEVERAL

A Van Fund was established in 1985 to obtain a Ford Super Wagon that seated fourteen passengers and a driver. The Seattle Foundation was especially helpful in obtaining this first NORSE HOME van. Other funds came from an unusual entertainment called "Vaudeville Extravaganza." Singing, dancing, comedy skits, recitations of poetry and "exotic" music played on rare instruments made up the Bill of Fare. Along with brave resident performers, the Administrator and department heads wore wild costumes and joined the fun. One skit featured Robert Solem playing himself as "an overwrought Administrator."

Several alterations were made to the new vehicle: installation of a permanent step with hand rails to allow passengers easy access; a lift for wheel chairs.

RESIDENT'S COUNCIL

The formation of a Resident's Council in October 1984 brought to the fore a clear voice from residents. It opened communication channels to staff and Board. Robert L. Surface, the Administrator of NORSE HOME at the time, wrote that the Council "serves as an aid to promote the welfare and happiness of the residents." The Resident's Council has been an active part of NORSE HOME ever since.

The Executive Committee of the NORSE HOME Resident's Council meets once a month. Its activities began in 1983, when meetings were held to discuss the purposes of such an organization and to draft By-Laws. On January 24, 1984, the first meeting of the Council was held. Officers were elected and By-Laws adopted. Later, sub-committees were formed. The Council acts as a helpful liaison between residents, the Board and the Administrator.

> The first officers of the new Resident's Council:
> Vic Sivertz – President
> Steve Smith – Vice President
> Edith Smith – Secretary
> Einer Nielsen – Treasurer

Every three months there is an open meeting of the Council for all residents, which includes a program or speaker. Besides Executive Committee officers, the meetings welcome comments and reports by the Administrator and Council chairpersons looking after Sunshine activities, the Libraries, the Social Hall, the preparation of biographies of new residents, and Sunday evening Vespers.

CHIT-CHAT — A RESIDENTS' PUBLICATION

In the 1980s, residents and staff produced a monthly publication called *Chit-Chat*. It was distributed to keep everyone informed about NORSE HOME activities. The Administrator usually contributed a column, as did volunteer organizations. Comments emerged from an Activities group, the Health Center (sometimes called "Nursing Notes"), Maintenance Department, Social Services, Laundry/Housekeeping/Custodial Services, Reception Desk, and Food Services Department — including hints on food items.

Chit-Chat also welcomed new residents with short biographies about them, thanked anyone who contributed to a festival, luncheon, meeting or other event, and advertised birthday greetings. It was not beyond *Chit-Chat* to insert poems or quips in its pages, many of them written by NORSE HOME residents. And occasional notes on interesting vacation trips appeared. One issue reminded residents of their Norse roots with heritage comments and recipes for Potato Lefse and Flatbrod. An editorial piece in 1994 was headed "What to Do in the Event of an Earthquake!" The short tongue-in-cheek answer: "Duck, Cover and Hold."

VESPER SERVICES

Each Sunday evening at 7:00 the Social Hall becomes an informal chapel. Visiting ministers from several denominations are invited. Attendees (parishioners) make contributions to cover the minister's fee and special music presentations, unless waived by the principals. Funds from those gifts have enabled the purchase of a Baldwin console piano and other amenities. NORSE HOME Guilds and Volunteer Auxiliary members help with the Vespers tradition.

FLAG-RAISING DAY AND DISTINGUISHED VISITORS

The day after the Twenty-Fifth Anniversary party, June 6, 1982, a flag-raising ceremony was held in the NORSE HOME garden. U.S. Senator Henry M. Jackson attended the event and noted that the new flag had flown over the Capitol in Washington, D.C., during the month of August 1981. Among those attending was Ed Mahlum, who designed NORSE HOME in the 1950s and had worked with Senator Jackson and others to obtain a FHA guaranteed loan to complete construction.

On October 28, 1983, H.H. Princess Astrid toured NORSE HOME, and another famous visitor was recorded in the Guest Book.

NEW POLICIES AND CHANGES

Besides capital improvements, NORSE HOME needed to improve the general atmosphere for residents, staff and visitors. Following are examples of those more subtle changes made during the 1980s:

SMOKE-FREE RESIDENCE

A "no smoking policy" was implemented by staff and department heads in 1988. Three reasons were given for the new policy: 1) Smoking is at odds with the health care mission of NORSE HOME; 2) Washington state legislation is pending on providing smoke-free environments for non-smokers; 3) Increasing numbers of court cases are winning the battle of making it the employer's responsibility to provide clean, safe workplaces. It was also revealed that a recent study indicated that accidents are more likely to happen to a smoker than to a non-smoker. Today NORSE HOME has a smoke-free building.

NATIONAL NURSING HOME WEEK

May 9-13, 1988, was recognized as National Nursing Home Week. (After the late 1980s, NORSE HOME was no longer described as a "Nursing Home." Under Administrator Robert Solem, its status changed from a "Skilled Nursing" facility to "Assisted Living.")

THE 1990s: QUEEN SONJA; THE 35TH BIRTHDAY PARTY; A REPLACEMENT VAN; BUILDING RENEWAL

REMODELED HEALTH CENTER

The third floor Health Center was a licensed, Skilled Nursing facility that had been Medicare certified since March 1982. The center included a second floor Residential Care Center. Every reasonable effort was made by staff to allow residents "to be just as independent as their physical or mental limitations will permit."

On July 15, 1991, bids were opened for a remodeling of NORSE HOME's Health Center. A friendly debate ensued.

One concern was that the price would be high due to equipment costs, fixtures for a new medication preparation room, a medical records office, a nutrition station and refurbishing public areas. Among special needs, carpeting would be chosen to replace the present vinyl tile, and new carpeting must accommodate maneuvering wheelchairs and reduce noise level.

Funds for the remodel came from the NORSE HOME Capital Improvement Fund, which depends on contributions and bequests from friends and supporters of NORSE HOME.

Assisted Living services are in place "for individuals who wish to maintain their independence while receiving the daily support they need." Trained caregivers are on duty 24 hours each day. The Assisted Living services include:

- Monitoring of health care needs
- Bathing and dressing assistance
- Personal hygiene and appearance

- Medication assistance and reminders
- Cognitive Support (perception)
- Laundry and housekeeping assistance
- Life enrichment activities and outings

ANOTHER ANNIVERSARY

NORSE HOME celebrated its 35th birthday on June 14, 1992, with harp music, raising the American flag (which had flown over our nation's Capitol building), a performance by the NORSE HOME Folk Dancers — including an original version of something called the "NORSE HOME Schottische." These events were topped off by an Open House from 2:30-4:00 PM.

NORSE HOME CLINIC

In April 1995, the new NORSE HOME Clinic opened for business. Located on the ground floor, the Clinic offered educational and social activities along with health care services and therapies. For example, Tai Chi classes were given (later dropped, then returned in 2010). Other treats included deep relaxation Sound Therapy, Jetta foot baths, Massage Therapy, and visits by physicians and dentists. Alternative medicine and herbal therapy were available.

NEW VAN

By summer 1995, over $67,000 had been raised — mostly by NORSE HOME residents — for a new van. It had larger capacity, easier passenger access, wider aisles, and a more efficient wheelchair lift than the previous van. Residents were again on the move.

ROYAL VISITOR

In late October 1995, Queen Sonja of Norway visited NORSE HOME. She could only afford an hour from her busy schedule (King Harald had appointments elsewhere), but upon her visit resident excitement was high and another famous signature appeared in the Guest Book.

BUILDING RENEWAL

In 1996, the NORSE HOME Board hired an independent firm to undertake a detailed study of the building. Four decades of use had left a few marks. Although substantial in every way, the safe and utilitarian building needed a makeover. During the 1990s over $3 million was spent on what was called an "Infrastructure Project." NORSE HOME was brought up to code and streamlined in several ways. For example, copper piping replaced old galvanized tubes; fire sprinklers were installed in resident apartments and public areas; efficient and brighter lighting illuminated everyone's days (and nights). In the late 1990s and in 2001, the second floor balcony was converted to an attractive dining and activity area for residents in the Assisted Living program. Other improvements: remodeling the dining room and entry way; lounge and reception areas received a makeover utilizing Nordic designs; the front lawn became a delightful Garden Court.

BED TAX AND A LITTLE POLITICS

In 1993, NORSE HOME residents, staff and others took up a lobbying effort in Olympia to stop proposed legislation to assess a three dollar per day fee per health center bed. The draft legislation was aimed at Washington State Continuing Care Retirement Centers (CCRCs). The proposal was heard but not approved by the House Revenue Committee. The NORSE HOME rally illustrated how senior citizens' voices can be raised — and heeded.

SALMON BARBECUES

Since the founding of NORSE HOME, annual Salmon Barbecues have drawn large crowds. This popular event was usually a cooperative arrangement between Ballard Oil Company and Lunde Electric Company. These two companies conducted barbecues for churches, clubs, lodges, Ballard Seafood Fest, senior citizen organizations and fishing vessel christenings.

Famous Pacific Northwest or Alaska salmon is usually barbecued over a green — or "wet" — alder fire. Large cookers are placed over the fires designed to hold fish at a proper level. The fillets are bedded in heavy aluminum handmade containers that hold a butter sauce mixture. Condiments are added as needed or requested. This feast is accompanied by scalloped potatoes, coleslaw and French bread. The NORSE HOME Salmon Barbecue has at times been held in local churches, including Ballard-First Lutheran Church and St. John Lutheran Church. Today NORSE HOME continues to provide this traditional event each September.

Board Of Trustees
Past and Present

PRESIDENTS OF THE BOARD OF TRUSTEES

NORSE HOME has been fortunate to have had outstanding leaders — Board, Staff, and Volunteers — since it opened for business in 1957.

To list everyone who made a difference is a large undertaking. Instead, following are names of the Board Presidents who steadied the NORSE HOME ship as she sailed into the twenty-first century.

1. Abraham Kvalheim, 1931-1940
2. Dr. T.W. Buschmann, 1941-1954
3. Paul P. Berg, 1955-1965
4. B. Thor Bjornstad, 1966-1968 and 1970-1973
5. Ole J. Adreasson, 1969
6. Albert Birkland, 1974-1976
7. Thor Ulvstad, 1977-1979
8. Peggy Stjern, 1980-1982
9. Trygve Kvalheim, 1983-1990 and 1996-1999
10. Trygve Jorgensen, 1991-1994
11. Wilbur Linde, 1994-1995
12. Bertil Lundh, 1995-1996
13. Henry Haugen, 1999-2006
14. Andrea Torland, 2007-2010
15. Konrad S.Uri, 2009-2013

(See Addendum II for Photos of Board of Trustees' Past Presidents)

HISTORICAL RECORD

In 1993, President of the Board Trygve Jorgensen suggested the creation of an official NORSE HOME historical record. Accordingly, he appointed Clarence "Pete" Pedersen and Thor Bjornstad to a new Historical Records Committee. Their job was to review loose archival material, much of which was in cardboard boxes, and purge this trove of extraneous and unimportant documents. Jorgensen asked anyone with "correspondence, newspaper articles or other material pertaining to NORSE HOME, past or present members of the Board of Trustees, past or present residents as well as past or present staff members" to turn over such material to members of the Historical Records Committee.

This book, a history of NORSE HOME and an overview of Norwegian immigration to Puget Sound, is in part a result of Trygve Jorgensen's 1993 decision to create an historical record. The 2012 book in your hand appeared with the encouragement of Konrad Uri, current President of the Board. Research and writing tasks were accomplished with volunteers and members of the wider community.

The Hands Of A Woman
Guilds and More: Creating Hospitality

WHAT IS A GUILD?

The role of women in the founding, operation and future of NORSE HOME has been immense. This chapter therefore cuts across the 50-year chronology of NORSE HOME to highlight the hands offered by talented and dedicated women at NORSE HOME. Although female volunteers and staff have always played key roles, the Guilds coalesced into an unusually active and interesting service army.

The word "Guild" came from the Middle Ages (500 to 1500 A.D.) and referred to an association of merchants or craftsmen. In current years a Guild has been defined as a "group of persons with common interests or aim for mutual aid and protection."

Taking a closer look, there is much more to a Guild than a brief dictionary reference. At NORSE HOME, these women's organizations have consistently met each month, staged gatherings, raised money, and helped write the history of a large retirement community on Seattle's Phinney Ridge.

THE NORWEGIAN HOSPITAL ASSOCIATION

Although not a NORSE HOME Guild, this organization set an example for other supporting organizations.

The Norwegian Hospital Association was formally established by six women on January 7, 1913, and incorporated in October of the same year. Its roots go back further — to a group called 'Barnevennen' (Children's Friend), founded on January 7, 1906.

The first formal meeting of the Association was held in Room 216 of the Seattle YMCA on November 5, 1913. Fourteen women attended. Marie (Mrs. Gunnar) Lund was elected president. Other officers: Vice President — Dina Kolderup; Secretary — Bernarda Lee Miller; Financial Secretary — Polla Strom Oleson; Treasurer — Carola Christy. Only eleven years later, December 1924, the hospital building was purchased at 3515 Woodland Park Avenue North, Seattle. Long before an image of NORSE HOME appeared on the horizon, the Association directly assisted Norwegian adults and children who were sick or otherwise in need of help.

Although not organized as a Guild (it preceded that activity), The Norwegian Hospital Association remained for many years the first and most consistent women's organization in support of NORSE HOME. When the Norwegian Hospital was forced to close, and the old building was sold, Association members continued to serve the Norwegian (and larger) community. After dissolution, the Association lent help to Children's Orthopedic Hospital. In 1941-1942, when NORSE HOME was struggling to emerge, the Association threw its resources and experience behind the new facility.

On October 17, 1994, the Association celebrated its 80th anniversary during a lunch in the NORSE HOME dining room. The Norwegian Hospital Association has disbanded, but it deserves to be remembered as the first organization of women that gave unstintingly to NORSE HOME.

ANNE MARIE FRODESEN STEINER

Norwegian-born Anne Marie Frodesen Steiner played key roles in both The Norwegian Hospital Association and the Guilds, especially the Guild named for her mother (Inga Frodesen). She was president of both organizations, but her involvements were wider: While becoming involved in NORSE HOME activities, she chaired the Edvard Grieg Festival Association, was vice-chair of the Seattle-Bergen Sister City Association, and was Associate Editor of *Ballard Voice* newspaper. She is also a Life Member of the Valkyrien Lodge, Daughters of Norway, and holds memberships in Leif Erikson Lodge, Sons of Norway, and the Norwegian Commercial Club. She is past president of The Norse Federation and served for many years on the Board of NORSE HOME. Anne Marie is a World War II veteran and served in the Norwegian and Danish sections of the Office of Strategic Services as a WAC in London.

THE ROLE OF WOMEN AT NORSE HOME

How things have changed. Or have they?

When The Norwegian Hospital Association and Guilds were on call for support of NORSE HOME, it was assumed by many that their members' roles would primarily consist of fundraising and social events. That assumption was only partly true. Guilds consistently, and for many years, filled in where others preferred not to tread.

A May 14, 1957 letter was sent from Dr. T.W. Buschmann's office at 630 Stimson Building, Seattle, signed by the "Ass't. Sec'y," to Mrs. Lew R. DeBritz, President of The Norwegian Hospital Association. It invited Association members to the May 26, 1957 NORSE HOME dedication, which was referred to in the letter as a "gala affair." The writer goes on: "Many dignitaries of the city and state will be present and we can expect a large crowd of people."

The letter continues: "Since the Guilds and the Norwegian Hospital Association are the back-bone of NORSE HOME, Inc. it would be nice if the ladies will serve as hostesses along with the Board members. We would appreciate very much having the ladies bring cookies. Coffee cake will be ordered, and if some groups prefer, they may donate toward the coffee cake instead of baking cookies."

WOMEN ON THE MOVE

Although spouses of Leif Erikson No. 1, Seattle, had been "aboard" the NORSE HOME project with their partners since the late 1920s, it wasn't until 1934 that an official "invitation" was sent to request participation of the Daughters of Norway lodges.

After the NORSE HOME, INC. organization was completed (1934), the corporation invited Daughters of Norway lodges to join the project. Specifically, the Daughters were asked to send representatives to the 1937 meeting of the Sons of Norway Home Corporation on June 19, 1937. Noted earlier, that meeting was re-scheduled for July 30, 1937, to give the Daughters of Norway lodges more time to consider the invitation.

At the July 30 meeting, several important steps were taken. The first was to change the name of the Corporation to "The NORSE HOME, Inc.," dropping the words "Sons of Norway Home." Another decision provided that Sustaining Members (those who contribute a specific amount of money) shall have the right to elect one-third of the members of the Board of Trustees; two-thirds to be elected by representatives of the Sons of Norway and the Daughters of Norway. The Sustaining Membership fee was fixed at a modest $5.00, and the Sustaining Life Membership fee at $100.00. Another change: the Board of Trustees was increased to nine members (later to 18). It was also decided that the location of NORSE HOME would be Seattle, Washington.

An important result of the last decision (i.e. location) was preparation of a contract to purchase a site. On August 2, 1939, a deed for the Phinney Ridge site was obtained by the Corporation.

THE GRAND LODGE, DAUGHTERS OF NORWAY, PACIFIC COAST

The NORSE HOME Review, a house publication designed to monitor the NORSE HOME fund raising campaign, was established in March, 1941. Albert S. Ryland was the Editor. The Review stated its purpose on its masthead: "Published monthly in the interest of THE NORSE HOME, INC. by the NORSE HOME Review Publishing Company, Bothell, Washington. Volume 1, Number 1 was of course filled with stories about NORSE HOME.

One Review piece was titled "Greetings from Grand President Gyda Christoferson." Mrs. Christoferson's words: "On behalf of the Grand Lodge, Daughters of Norway, on the Pacific Coast, I extend to you my sincere wishes for every success for your new publication, the "NORSE HOME Review." (And, by implication, Mrs. Christoferson is wishing success to NORSE HOME.)

The same edition of the Review contained a story titled "Purpose of Sons and Daughters of Norway Orders." The unnamed writer states: "We believe that the particular purpose of these Orders is to acquaint their members, children, and other Americans of Norse blood with Norway and Norwegian achievements and thereby make them conscious and proud of their Norse ancestry... Our special mission as Sons and Daughters of Norway is to see to it that Americans of Norse descent are informed of the ideals and the achievements so that they become conscious, happy and proud of their Norse ancestry and will strive to perpetuate the ideals of that ancestry in our great American nation."

The Review notes the following women as Trustees of the NORSE HOME Corporation: Mrs. Severin Anderson, Mrs. Kristine Aspen, Mrs. Marie Berglund, Mrs. Hannah Heglund, Mrs. Sefferine Krogstad and Mrs. Magnhild Rostad. Although composing a minority of the Board, women had established their presence on NORSE HOME's governing council.

INGA HUMLEBEKK FRODESEN (1888-1963)

Dr. Trygve W. Buschmann, in his first year as President of NORSE HOME, Inc., called a special meeting on March 28, 1941 to discuss NORSE HOME Guilds. Dr. Buschmann asked Mrs. Inga Frodesen to undertake that task. As the record indicates, she did so with dedication and hard work. In later years, she was informally and affectionately called "Mother of NORSE HOME."

Inga Humlebekk came to America in 1909. Like many of her friends and neighbors she became active in supporting organizations with Norwegian roots, especially the Daughters of Norway. On a return visit to Norway (which many immigrants did after establishing themselves in the New World) she met her future husband, Frode Frodesen.

Mr. Frodesen, then a young bricklayer, came to America via Vancouver, B.C., Canada, in 1905. He arrived soon after the earthquake in San Francisco, where he had moved to help rebuild that damaged city. Inga and Frode were married in the Stewart home on Vashon Island, Washington, a short ferry ride from southwest Seattle. Inga was a much-loved "au pair" of the Stewart children in this island community. In time, Frode became a highly respected mason contractor, building schools and churches on the West Coast in partnership with his son, Fred (Olav). Son John became a general contractor. Their office building (F. Frodesen Masonry and Farwest Construction) was in Ballard, not far from NORSE HOME.

Using Daughters of Norway lodges and members as contacts, Inga Frodesen traveled the State of Washington during the 1940s. Her organizational talents and gracious charm resulted in the creation of twenty-five active Guilds. Several Guilds dropped out over time, but for many years about nineteen Guilds could be counted on to help sustain NORSE HOME. In 2012, two Guilds remain active: Inga Frodesen and Seterjenten.

In 1960, a written tribute to Inga Frodesen, who had been ill for some time, noted that when she "entered the (Daughters) Lodge Hall a feeling of good will prevailed... her beautiful poems and her writings about her beloved Norway (were) an inspiration... she gave unselfishly of her time and talent, for the benefit of the suffering and the sorrowful."

THE FIRST GUILD

Most of the Guilds were formed by women with common backgrounds and interests. With Inga Frodesen's help, in spring 1941, the first Guild was formed by Mrs. Ludvig Uri. It took the name "Sunroom" because the members chose to build and furnish a "sunny recreation place at NORSE HOME".

SPEAKING OUT

Representatives of the Guilds were not timid about raising funds, hosting events, or asking questions.

An example: Mrs. L.R. Ottesen, writing the Board of Directors on behalf of the Seterjenten Guild, noted that the campaign had slowed — she used the term "standstill" (early 1950s). Citing costs over the years, Mrs. Ottesen asked why the building goal had gone from $150,000 to $200,000 to $400,000. "Where will this all end up?" she asked.

NORSE HOME VOLUNTEER AUXILIARY

In the 1940s and 1950s — and beyond — Guilds were the key to many important events. As Guilds disbanded, residents and friends of NORSE HOME suggested a Volunteer Auxiliary to supplement Guild work and to take on projects such as the Twenty-Fifth Anniversary Celebration in 1982.

The Auxiliary was founded on November 4, 1981. June Bjornstad (sister-in-law of Thor Bjornstad and wife of Board of Trustees President Trygve Bjornstad) was its first chair. Charter members were Else Bentsen, Della Comfort, Dorothy DeTree, Dordi Nord, Gudrun Ofstad, Inger Olsen, and Emma Varney (mother of resident Myrtle Varney).

Perhaps the main Auxiliary event, with assistance from Guild members, was the Annual Holiday Bazaar. The Bazaar features hand-crafted items, Christmas ornaments, and home-made cookies and breads. Virtually all goodies for sale have a Nordic connotation, which makes them especially attractive to both Scandinavian and non-Scandinavian customers.

SKILLS AND NEEDS

Among needs identified for volunteers are direct service to patients in the nursing center; assisting with writing letters, or taking residents on shopping, medical and entertainment excursions. These and other volunteer contributions are organized and monitored. For example, the NORSE HOME Volunteer Auxiliary is treated as a professional group. Individual skills are evaluated and deployed, and time sheets are kept.

GUILD ROLL CALL

Many Guilds remained active into the 1980s. Others, due to retirement or passing of members left the scene. Specific activities of Guilds are described below in the section titled: WHAT DO GUILDS ACCOMPLISH?

SETERJENTEN	PHINNEY
INGA FRODESEN	FREYA
SUNSET HILL	SYNNOVE SOLBAKKEN
SOLVEIG	HARMONY
KETCHIKAN	FAGERHEIM
WOODLAWN	STAR
MIDNATSOL	SOLGLIMT
YOU AND I	WEST SEATTLE SOLGLIMT
NORONNA	FOUR LEAF CLOVER
CARLETON PARK	NORSE HOME (Spokane, Washington)
SUNROOM	FEMBORINGEN

To thank these groups, several NORSE HOME friends have written about Guild accomplishments. For instance, Anne Marie Frodesen Steiner, daughter of Inga Frodesen, wrote in gratitude: "Every Guild has donated to the Building Fund and gave (the Fund) a big life when it was most needed. Everyone had their own project to work for, but when the money was needed to keep the men working after the contract was let (to build NORSE HOME), they felt the call to give and (were) proud..."

Soon after organization of the Guilds, a Memorial Fund was started to remember Guild members who labored in love for NORSE HOME.

DEPENDABLE PARTNERS

The following organizations, other than Guilds, have been consistent over many years in providing long-term or last-minute help to NORSE HOME. Many other groups from the wider world have generously donated time and money, and NORSE HOME appreciated help from every responsible source. However, to list every supporter for what many thought was an impossible undertaking would require a second volume to this story. It's fair to say that, besides Guilds, the following organizations have been dependable friends.

NORWEGIAN HOSPITAL ASSOCIATION
VALKIRIEN LODGE, DAUGHTERS OF NORWAY
LEIF ERIKSON LODGE, SONS OF NORWAY
SUNNMORSLAGET av SEATTLE
NORDLANDSLAGET
NORWEGIAN COMMERCIAL CLUB
NORSE HOME BINGO CLUB
KNUTE ROCKNE LODGE, SONS OF NORWAY
NORWEGIAN MALE CHORUS
NORWEGIAN LADIES CHORUS
HELPMATES FOR NORWEGIAN MALE CHORUS

And there are many more partners. Because the rolls of NORSE HOME donors and helpmates are extraordinarily long, and dominated by obscure names, one is reminded of Benjamin Franklin's words:

"A man is sometimes more generous when he has but a little money than when he has plenty, perhaps thro' fear of being thought to have but little."

WHAT DO GUILDS ACCOMPLISH?

Guild activity moved to high gear immediately after joining the initial fundraising Campaign, and remained busy long after NORSE HOME was built. Many Guild contributions to NORSE HOME have been special and permanent.

Several Guilds closed their activities after members retired or passed on. It was also difficult to recruit members' daughters, nieces or granddaughters when the general employment of women increased in the 1950s. The remaining Guilds continue to fill a large role ensuring community involvement in occasional special projects and celebrations.

Examples of Guild Contributions:

Funds were raised from an early style show and dinner at Norway Hall, 2015 Boren Avenue, Seattle. Mrs. Norris Finnestad was in charge, with assistance from Mrs. Carl Sather of Solveig Guild, Mrs. Ragnar Svendsen representing Seterjenten Guild, and Mrs. Ole Birkvold of Midnatsol Guild. (One of the founding members of Midnatsol Guild was Mrs. Emma C. Uri, mother of current Board President, Konrad S. Uri.) Models in the children's section included Ingri Stang, daughter of the Norwegian Consul, Margot Waale, and Ann Carlson.

To celebrate its fortieth anniversary, Midnatsol Guild on April 10, 1984 hosted a luncheon in NORSE HOME's Social Hall. Members were reminded of the need for Senior Citizens retirement homes with appropriate comforts and health care. Members reminisced about their years of activities: cookie sales, garden sales, luncheons. Until the Guild went out of business, it arranged an annual Christmas party for patients in the Health Center.

Solveig Guild activities were similar to Midnatsol's: bazaars and luncheons, but Solveig also specialized in organizing raffles. Solveig Guild was organized at the home of Mrs. Severin Andersen on September 23, 1941. In the 1940s and 1950s, members did something unusual: They toured other retirement homes in search of ideas for NORSE HOME.

To honor the "Mother" of the Guilds and NORSE HOME, Inga Frodesen Guild was organized in January 1960. The Guild remains active (2012) and meets every fourth Monday at NORSE HOME. Another treat is the Guild's freshly baked Valentine waffles which are served to all residents in the Dining Hall. Every May members make a financial contribution to NORSE HOME honoring their founder, Inga Frodesen, on her birthday (May 13). This Guild held the first Salmon Barbecue at NORSE HOME — now a tradition — on November 1, 1968. Another project is the annual Christmas Luncheon and Auction — always well attended. Most Guilds have donated funds to art and music. For example, the Inga Frodesen Guild helped buy the piano in the Social Hall and the painted mural by Guild member Melissa Koch in the Coffee Lounge.

Alaskans are sometimes put out of mind because NORSE HOME is Seattle-based. An important reminder of Alaska's support of NORSE HOME is the Ketchikan Guild. This Guild was founded on March 13, 1947, with Alvilda Stamas Larsen at the helm. Each member was from or had lived for a time in Ketchikan, Alaska.

Seterjenten Guild was founded in 1941, the fourth Guild to be organized in support of NORSE HOME. During the war, many of its members had jobs, so meetings were held in the evening. The "Seterjenten Soup Supper" is a Guild special event. The Guild is also known for its silent auctions and luncheons. Guild members provided flags to be flown over NORSE HOME. Recently, the Guild provided funding for the Concierge's desk in the main lobby.

Another early Guild, Sunset Hill, was founded in 1941. It was the third Guild to be organized. Their main fundraiser for years was a luncheon and afternoons of playing bridge.

- Femboringen Guild, organized on September 18, 1978, by Haldis Jules and Emma Varney, collaborated with the J.C. Penney Company to stage fashion shows. Penney's fashion staff fitted the models' clothes, provided training and hair-styling, and applied make-up. Guild members handled decorating and set-up, and provided homemade refreshments for these popular shows. Femboringen fundraising projects also included Champagne suppers and musical evenings. Winnie Pedersen (Mrs. Clarence), a longtime member of Femboringen, kept a record of the Guild's donations. Examples: on October 9, 1991, it contributed $1,000 for renovation of the third floor; on April 17, 1995, $1,000 was given to the Van (car) Fund; during 1997, the Guild raised $1,350 for the purchase of a piano for the Social Hall.

- Woodlawn Guild was founded in 1941, and Guild members met in private homes on the third Thursday of each month. Lunch was served and bridge games were arranged. Upon celebrating the Guild's 59th Anniversary, a tea was served at NORSE HOME in April 1991.

- Harmony Guild gave an organ to NORSE HOME in June, 1957. The NORSE HOME Board of Directors also thanked the Guild for donating cookies, money and hosting help at the NORSE HOME dedication on May 26, 1957, at which the NORSE HOME front door was opened with a Gold Key held by General Contractor P.D. Wick.

Anne Marie Frodesen Steiner remembers a galaxy of gifts from Guilds to NORSE HOME. Several of those items are listed here in no particular order:

Wheel Chairs	Folding Chairs
Large Garden	PlantsCard Tables
Large Food	CartElectric Range (Social Hall)
Song Book	Furniture Recovering
Dishwasher	Nursing Center Equipment
Dishware	

And perhaps most importantly, Guilds continue to donate funds to the NORSE HOME Resident Assistance Fund (formerly known as the Endowment Fund).

ANNA'S INVESTMENT

ANNA and HARALD LARSSEN virtually grew up with NORSE HOME in their back yard. Each of their two homes had oblique, distant views of Phinney Ridge looming over Scandinavian Ballard. Resting next to Woodland Park, NORSE HOME became part of the LARSSEN family's heritage. After HARALD had carried his tool box in and out of the NORSE HOME for years, ANNA made her decision. Improving her rosemaling and painting was important, but contributing to the Norwegian tradition of helping others made sense. After all, many strangers had helped her and HARALD adapt to America. Her investment in NORSE HOME was through membership in an active Guild. She chose Femboringen, in part because she had enjoyed several NORSE HOME musical events sponsored by that Guild. ANNA also chose Femboringen because her nursing profession had taken up so many hours of her work day she wanted to make a different kind of contribution. Once or twice a month, ANNA drove up to the Ridge or to a Guild member's home, and accepted any responsibility the Guild assumed. With her and HARALD's children taking care of themselves, the world of NORSE HOME Guilds was a perfect fit for the LARSSEN family.

Chapter V. An Interactive Community

"There's No Place Like NORSE HOME"

(NORSE HOME Brochure 2012)

Anna's Fifth Letter

Dear Family,

Harald and I don't rush about anymore, but we are healthy. Harald claims
he is retired, but nothing stops him from working on projects, collecting
books, or coming up with ideas for weekend trips. He thinks it's time
to move into the NORSE HOME, the large retirement community I have told
you about. I'm not sure. My house and garden give me so much pleasure.
Another complication is that I have converted our guest room into a
complete sewing and rosemaling headquarters. So despite the fact that
we have many friends at NORSE HOME, and Phinney Ridge provides one of
Seattle's best four-way views, I'm reluctant to make a big change during
my last year of nursing. But who knows what the next year or so will
bring? In other news, our son Hal, his wife and two children seem to
enjoy our company. They join us for dinner or a visit to Woodland Park
almost every two weeks. Mari has not married and she rarely visits
Seattle. She likes Minneapolis, Minnesota where she works in biological
research for the University of Minnesota and does volunteer work at The
Walker Art Center, mostly at the Sculputure Garden. This weekend Harald
and I will board the ferry in Seattle and visit his first American home
in Poulsbo, Washington. There are good bookstores in that little port
town and it also has one of the best bakeries. Harald has stayed in touch
with a couple of old friends across Puget Sound, one of whom lives in a
retirement home called Martha and Mary. Last May 17 we marched in the
Norwegian Constitution parade in downtown Ballard. Harald did fine, but
I left after four or five blocks to find a coffee shop and rest my feet.
Thank you for your wonderful birthday gifts. Anything from Norway is very
exciting.

Anna

Harald's Fifth Letter

To everyone at home,

Today I found two old books in Norwegian about Haugesund. One was very expensive. I also bought a history of our Saami friends and a respected noaide, or shaman, who defended those people. You will remember how we visited Saami communities up north when we were very young? I'll add these books to my library. If my kids don't want them I know several Norwegian libraries in Ballard, including one at NORSE HOME that might like them. Two weeks ago I helped finish a cedar canoe for Indians who operate a cultural center at an old U.S. Army post in Seattle called Fort Lawton. The Daybreak Star Center is open to everyone, but members of local Native tribes are in charge. The boat, with a fierce animal design on the prow, is on display outside the center's entrance. I helped shape the canoe, but Indians did the design and colorful decorations. Next year Anna and I will make a decision about our future. I'd like to live in smaller quarters, but with enough room for my books. Anna doesn't want to give up her garden and neighborhood. Maybe our kids will have an opinion? Anna and I attend Sunday services at Phinney Ridge Lutheran Church. It is almost next door to NORSE HOME, which I have told you about. Anna's old church, Immanuel Lutheran, is still active near downtown Seattle but it has changed into more of a service center for homeless people. Anna's favorite minister at Immanuel Lutheran, Hans Stub, retired and died many years ago. I was sorry to hear about several funerals in Haugesund, but thanks for sending us the notices. This afternoon Anna and I do our weekly shopping at a huge local supermarket. It takes us forty-five minutes or an hour to wheel our basket up and down every aisle. Although you — and certainly Oslo — have larger food markets today, you would not believe the size of American stores.

Harald

Practicing The Tradition
Today and Tomorrow

Today NORSE HOME is a Retirement and Assisted Living community. The affordable independent living apartments have the comfort of community living where monthly rents include 24-hour security, all meals (and lots of special events), laundry and housekeeping, all utilities including Internet service and cable TV. Under the Washington State Department of Social and Health Services (DSHS) Boarding home laws, when the need arises, personal assistance and 24-hour nursing services are available for all activities of daily living.

In the beginning the need for "an old folks home" was behind the thrust of activity to create the NORSE HOME. It was built with the sturdy safe structure, open common areas and individual "bedroom" apartments. With elevators and a central telephone system, it resembled a grand hotel where elders could rent an apartment to be in a safe and secure environment among friends. The third floor was known as the "infirmary." This would later become the Skilled Nursing Floor.

NORSE HOME always looked after all of its residents' care needs, but in the early 1990s the Department of Health's new laws for all senior housing properties created a new license that was necessary to care for residents at a lower level of need than Skilled Nursing. This was the emergence of the Assisted Living industry, requiring a boarding home license and regulated first by the Department of Health and currently by DSHS.

NORSE HOME was one of the first in the Seattle area to then have all three services available under one roof (Independent Living, Assisted Living and Skilled Nursing). The term for NORSE HOME and other properties with these three levels of care became known as a CCRC, or a Continuing Care Retirement Community.

NORSE HOME leadership foresaw the ever-increasing complexities of the health care bureaucracy and opted to assure the comfort and home-like setting for end of life care. The Skilled Nursing facility was replaced with greater Assisted Living capacity. This transfer to AL status occurred in February, 2008. The third floor nursing station remains as the hub of the home for those with greater needs.

NORSE HOME has distinguished itself in lay and professional communities as a highly preferred home-like setting for hospice care. The warm and caring staff is recognized by others for providing high quality individualized service, and is one of the few Assisted Living properties in the Seattle area with a licensed nurse on-site 24 hours a day.

In August of 2012 NORSE HOME completed another milestone. The fourth floor has had necessary updates to allow Assisted Living services for those Independent Living residents in need of services, without their having to move to a different floor. The NORSE HOME's long-range plan is to offer this option on the fifth and sixth floors also. This will make NORSE HOME up-to-date with the newer Assisted Living properties in the city.

NORSE HOME continues to be a "home for life."

Programs, Events And Traditions
What is an Amenity?

The small pleasures and habits of life become more important in our later years. Since the doors opened in 1957, NORSE HOME has strived each year to create a living environment that is calm, physically attractive, affordable, convenient, and safe. These conditions are achieved through staff professionalism, suggestions from residents and guests, and the good old learning curve.

NORSE HOME representatives have participated in seminars, visited other similar facilities, and listened to comments from visitors and residents. Besides the accepted and expected amenities — such as pleasant and accessible dining facilities; comfortable living and socializing spaces; nearby laundry rooms; men's and women's hair salon; and useful libraries — NORSE HOME also has a wellness clinic; an exercise room with trained Restorative Aides on duty; a Seamstress on staff; and a host of transportation drivers. A passenger car and a 15-passenger van escort residents to medical appointments, shopping sprees, the beach, to see the tulips in Skagit Valley in the spring, to local ballroom dance classes, and many other places of interest near and far. The staff and residents are interactive. There is a regular Vesper service each Sunday evening. Residents assist with each visiting pastor.

With an outdoor patio and spectacular views from every window, NORSE HOME also offers a few additional pleasant surprises.

GARDEN COURT

The errant duck and bird have occasionally found the little pond and greenery perfect for a vacation or casual home. The patio embraces trees, shrubs and a flower garden that, on a small scale, rival attractions of nearby Woodland Park. The historic NORSE HOME Cornerstone is nearby, which reminds everyone when and why NORSE HOME joined its Phinney Ridge neighbors in the 1950s. Of course, it also holds founders' names.

When the original building was planned, it was agreed by architects and the NORSE HOME Board that construction should occupy virtually every foot of space between Phinney and Greenwood Avenues and North 54th and North 53rd Streets. The Garden Court was therefore almost an afterthought. It was first used as a staging area for construction equipment, later as "open space" (hosting the occasional gathering).

In 2001, this precious area was transformed into a natural resting area for human beings — and the occasional wildlife representative — to enjoy Seattle's unpredictable weather. The "new" Garden Court includes landscaping, a stone fountain made from Norwegian granite, a verdant barrier of trees and hedges, and the centerpiece fishpond.

SOOTHING THE SENSES

Following a period of what might be called "spaciousness" within the building, art works, color patterns and coordinated designs began to evolve within the interior. It became clear that human expression of the senses needed more recognition.

NORSE HOME art consists of mostly donated paintings, prints, reproductions, tapestries, embroideries, and carvings. Money is periodically found to clean and restore art works.

In 1992, Board President Trygve Jorgensen appointed an Art Committee to evaluate and oversee the growing collection. This led to a more organized effort to appreciate and care for the changing colors and shapes watching over residents, staff and guests.

Carvings by Olaf Hagen from Trondheim, Norway, can be appreciated, including his wooden sculpture surrounding a valuable Seth Thomas clock, and a tall chest in the dining room holding rich, detailed designs.

Paintings adorn the walls of every corridor. These art displays are a mix of casual resident works; original pieces by former NORSE HOME resident and prolific painter Carl Knudsen; and anonymous portraits of Nordic figures and Scandinavian landscapes. One source of these art works is water-color and drawing classes conducted at NORSE HOME.

Several other unusual visual expressions greet viewers. One is the large color photo of Norway's King Olav V. Another is a painting of musician Ole Bornemann Bull.

OLE BULL'S PORTRAIT

The Ole Bull portrait in the Fireplace Lounge often draws comment. The story of Bull is an unusual tale. Although Ole Bull had passed on before NORSE HOME existed, his reputation as a musical genius, flamboyant personality, and Norwegian patriot made him a familiar figure among Scandinavians.

A child prodigy, Bull was admitted to the Bergen orchestra as first violinist when he was eight years old. He personally knew Schumann, Liszt and Wagner. Hans Christian Anderson used Bull as a "fairy prince" in his writings. Some historians believe that Bull's extraordinary life inspired Ibsen's classic Peer Gynt.

Although Bull became well known in European capitals and in Moscow, North Africa, and of course Scandinavia, he spent the 1860s – 1870s in America. He frequently toured the Mid-west — home to thousands of Norwegians — giving concerts and lectures. Bull's efforts to create "Oleana," a Pennsylvania-based utopian Norwegian colony, failed. He and his followers later admitted that the maestro was, after all, a musician, not a businessman.

CELEBRATIONS

The brightly colored, newly furnished and renovated NORSE HOME is always eager to show off its improvements and décor. Although traditional celebrations have always been part of the monthly and yearly life of residents and staff, after the 1998 renovation a renewed effort was launched to welcome "everyone" to see and enjoy NORSE HOME's rebirth.

Of course, May 17 (*Syttende Mai*), Norwegian Constitution Day, is given full-blown expression, including a NORSE HOME presence in the May 17 parade in Ballard. NORSE HOME seasonal and national lunches and dinners have become well-known Seattle events. These feasts, or Smorgasbords, provide historical delicacies such as *Lutefisk*, *Krumkake*, *Lefse*, *Surkal* (sauerkraut), *Rodkal* (red cabbage), pickled herring, Swedish meatballs, and smoked salmon.

Additionally, there are the monthly Sunday brunch buffets, the Potato Ball (a specialty dinner held in the spring) and the *Julebord* in December. And, as part of the NORSE HOME tradition, there is a Leif Erikson Day recognition. Of course, American national holidays have full-blown, enthusiastic programs, and even Groundhog Day is remembered.

50TH ANNIVERSARY CELEBRATION

NORSE HOME's 50th Anniversary Celebration was held the weekend of June 15, 16, and 17, 2007. A number of programs were held to recognize the 50th. A five-course dinner was served to residents and their families; Harpist John Harrington and pianist Carol Buschmann provided musical interludes; the Royal Norwegian Vice Consul Kim Nesselquist was present; and former Board members gathered for an historical overview. A memorable highlight was the accordion music and humorous comments of Seattle's famous Scandinavian performer, Stan Boreson.

REACHING OUT

As the initial NORSE HOME campaign got under way in the 1940s – 1950s, a gentle "Norwegian flood tide" was underway in the Queen City.

For example, in the late 1950s, a radio program called *The Scandinavian Hour* was established. Today this popular weekly broadcast includes conversations and announcements regarding NORSE HOME happenings.

Longevity

Staff and Residents

STAFF

Throughout this history we have learned about how NORSE HOME came to be, the vision of its founders, and the progression of time it took to have the idea, raise the funds and build the actual property. It is noteworthy to mention those who continue this mission and those who benefit from the vision.

When the doors opened in 1957, the working staff was estimated to have been about 24. The 116 "inaugural" group of residents who moved into NORSE HOME during 1957 were more independent, and the overall needs of the property were not as great as they are today. At that time staff, under the direction of an Administrator, took care of the business of renting apartments, screening new residents, preparing and serving meals in one dining room, as well as housekeeping duties and maintaining a new building—and those original boilers! The Board of Trustees, as volunteers, also took on many roles for the daily needs of maintaining and developing the service needs of the property. The Guilds, as we have learned, kept up with the hospitality events with all the coffee and cookies.

Because over the years the laws have changed, staffing changes have occurred. Today there is staff on property 24-hours a day seven days a week. The night shift includes licensed nurses and resident assistants in nursing and building services for security. At all times the Health Services department cares for residents receiving Assisted Living services and is available for emergencies for all residents who are not. The Wellness Clinic is also managed by a licensed nurse and helps coordinate wellness opportunities for the more independent residents.

The trained Restorative Aides manage the Fitness Center giving residents full opportunity for mobility and strength improvements.

The Activities Department offers a wide variety of programs enabling all to keep up with their previous hobbies or find new ones. In addition to art classes that produce award-winning pieces, there are many group activities for mental and physical exercises. These include the nationally recognized lively and interactive EnhanceFitness Program. The now famous Readers' Theatre, an original production, is written and directed by the Activities Coordinator and performed by NORSE HOME residents. It has been delighting audiences for over 19 years.

NORSE HOME is known for its quality and quantity of home-style meals, including many Scandinavian favorites. The dietary staff prepares meals and serves three dining rooms.

The new NORSE HOME Catering Department offers a full menu for individual meals delivered to your home or group events.

The Building Services department, which includes both housekeeping and maintenance, assists residents daily. Housekeepers personalize their service to fit residents' needs, while keeping all common areas sparkling. The maintenance group completes daily work orders for residents, which include moving furniture, hanging pictures, and other requests as needed. It is also their responsibility to assist in updating the historic building inside and out.

The Administrative staff begins with the friendly welcome from the front desk. The Resident Services Director, a Social Worker (MSW), assists those interested in becoming a new resident, while others assist with community outreach, marketing, human resources, business management and development, personal transportation and seamstress services. The Executive Director (formerly known as the Administrator) manages this devoted group of 92 who work the revolving 24/7 schedule.

The current Executive Director, Jennifer Jorgensen, also has loyalty and legacy. Her father, Trygve Jorgensen, mentioned on earlier pages, was a past President of the Board of Trustees. To bring things current, under her guidance more efficient working spaces have been created, and new programs have been developed to comply with Assisted Living practices. This includes the installation of electronic record keeping.

A private family dining room was built to provide residents with an opportunity to host their own private family dinner or meeting. As a visionary, the Executive Director has anticipated upcoming and future needs for the NORSE HOME to be competitive in the local senior housing marketplace and to meet the potential wants and needs of the aging "boomer" population. Recently, Jennifer has organized the plans and established the capability of Flex Licensing on the fourth, fifth, and sixth floors. For community outreach, there is a new NORSE HOME Catering Department that now also offers home delivery.

There is longevity among the NORSE HOME staff. It is a remarkable testimony to the mission and vision of NORSE HOME that there are staff members who have continually worked for the NORSE HOME. There are 13 employees with over five years of service, 22 with over 10, nine with over 20, and even a couple with over 35 years.

Another remarkable fact is that some of these staff members who have started out at an entry level position in the Dietary Department and Custodial Department have, through educational opportunities, been advanced and were hired in other departments. Examples include one individual who began in dietary, became a CNA, (Certified Nursing Assistant), and now is a Licensed Nurse. Others who started out in Dietary went on to be trained as administrative assistants, receptionists, human resource manager, and building services maintenance professionals. There is even one who started out in

Custodial and was trained and became proficient in Senior Living Activities. In reviewing old Board of Trustees' meeting minutes it is also true that previous administrators had advanced from other positions in the NORSE HOME.

ROBERT SOLEM, Ph.D.

Robert Solem, who held the NORSE HOME Administrator's position from 1985 to 2007, was the longest serving administrator. It was during his tenure that NORSE HOME became licensed as an Assisted Living property in addition to being a retirement community. Mr. Solem's accounting background helped him work through the complicated tasks of establishing monthly rental fees, founder fees and service fees versus a daily rate system. In addition to witnessing many changes over the years, he was often seen interacting with residents and even took a part in the famous NORSE HOME Reader's Theatre performances.

By the way, not all staff are Norwegian. In fact, a recent researcher learned there are 17 countries represented by this remarkable staff. The respect for each other is shared at an annual staff event, which is a multi-cultural potluck feast. What this staff shares, it seems, is a humble, good-hearted attitude. The visible interaction with residents is obvious when you walk in the front door.

RESIDENTS

..."the combination of friendly informality and yet efficiency often takes me back to a time when the world somehow seemed more in harmony with the best in the human spirit. My family is very grateful."*

— Family of a NORSE HOME Resident, 2012

In the beginning and in the end, it is all about the RESIDENTS. It is what the property was built for and it is who the property serves. Whereas, the NORSE HOME was originally founded to serve the vast Norwegian population in the Seattle area, today it proudly states that it offers, "Scandinavian hospitality to an International population." Among the residents, there are currently at least 10 homeland countries represented. Perhaps it is the overall feeling of knowing that others have "old country" ties that bond residents with each other and with the staff regardless of their "old country."

Again, the residents have a remarkable NORSE HOME history. It is testimonial to carrying out the mission and vision of the NORSE HOME founders that many who worked so hard to bring this property to fruition have gone on to be a part of the community and enjoy the hospitality it provides.

It is not possible to write about all the resident stories that have occurred in the last 55 years. However, here are a few examples to share with you.

Even though founders August and Dr. T.W. Buschmann did not become residents at the NORSE HOME, we know that of their other seven siblings, at least five of their relatives did reside at NORSE HOME, three of them all at the same time in the late 1970s. There is still a Buschmann presence at NORSE HOME today. The safe belonging to Dr. T.W. Buschmann can be seen in the Founders Room. Carol Buschmann and Noreen Buschmann Jacky, the great nieces of August and Dr. T.W. Buschmann (their grandfather was a brother, Eigil Buschmann), still perform in their musical group for the residents and families of NORSE HOME each December during the holiday season.

You have read about Thor Bjornstad, who was one of those instrumental in getting the NORSE HOME built. He not only was present at the ground breaking, but he and much of his family eventually lived at NORSE HOME. The longevity of family history and the lives of its residents is a big part of NORSE HOME history.

Susan Bjornstad Brown (who was delivered by Dr. T.W. Buschmann) recently shared some of this family history. Her father had nine siblings. She is the daughter, niece and cousin of many of the former residents and of one current resident. There were five members of her family living here at one time. Her aunt Lilly Bjornstad lived here until she was 109. When the Queen of Norway came to visit the NORSE HOME, she was selected to present the Queen with flowers. When asked by a local newspaper why she thought she was chosen, she quickly replied, "because I am the oldest person here." Susan's mother and father, Trygve (former Board President) and his wife, Gertrude "Tootsie" Bjornstad, moved to the NORSE HOME. Her Uncle Thor and his wife, June Bjornstad, also moved to NORSE HOME. As is true today, often couples would decide to move to NORSE HOME when they no longer wanted to prepare meals or have to keep up a large home, or one person of the couple was in need of assistance. It is reported that when the brothers Bjornstad moved to NORSE HOME, they went to the kitchen and "requested there would be potatoes and gravy at every dinner." In the early days there was also the desire to socialize or "party" with family and friends easily. The Bjornstad family gave much of their time and resources to continue the longevity and legacy of the NORSE HOME.

Susan also has the connection to Ole L. Ejde, who was the Editor of the *Washington-Posten*. He was her maternal grandfather. We have read on earlier pages his significance and how he greatly promoted the NORSE HOME. Susan remembers how the care and caring of the NORSE HOME definitely were responsible for her family members living longer and happier lives. Today, Susan visits her cousin Lucille Hayes at the NORSE HOME.

Lucille Hayes, daughter of Lilly and Andrew Bjornstad, has been a resident at the NORSE HOME since 1998. She recalled her own adjustment to America. Her Norwegian-born parents were sensitive and slightly embarrassed about their accents. The family found comfort — and recreation — and walked everywhere. Seattle treks to Golden Gardens and Woodland Park became routine. Lucille also recalls her mother's devotion to opera, which was appreciated by the entire family. Her Bjornstad relatives successfully made the transition from Old World to New, and many of them lived in and helped guide the development of NORSE HOME.

Myrtle Varney is currently proud to be the third generation to live in the same apartment at NORSE HOME. Born in 1927, Ms. Varney recalls her youthful days exploring Woodland Park. Of course, she saw NORSE HOME physically rise before her eyes. She knew the animals in the zoo; watched the Ferris wheel burn to the ground; remembered a violin shop next door to the Ferris wheel; and consumed hamburgers at a favorite restaurant on Fremont Avenue. When Aurora Avenue was built through Woodland Park (1932), she was horrified, as were many Seattle residents. As a young woman in her 30s, she bicycled to NORSE HOME, where "Grandma Larson" lived. For a period she lived in Guy Phinney's former home on Fremont Avenue — a building, she recalled, constructed with hand-made nails.

Later, during her married life, she lived in West Seattle for forty years. However, Myrtle Varney's memories of Woodland Park and NORSE HOME never disappeared. She is now (2012) "back home," active in the life and rhythms of NORSE HOME. Perhaps she may soon publish a volume of her poetry with references to her rich Seattle life.

Another story with longevity roots involves Emma Vatn. Emma is currently a resident at NORSE HOME but tells how she remembers being at the NORSE HOME ground breaking in December 1955.

There are currently residents who had been active Guild members in the past; who worked hard with their Femboringen Guild's fundraisers to help the residents. When Winnie Peterson moved to NORSE HOME in 2012, two of her daughters had mothers-in-law living at NORSE HOME already. Solveig Berg and her late husband, Thor, a former member of the Board of Trustees, moved to NORSE HOME in 2007.

Additional past NORSE HOME Board Members have been moving in. For example, Lila Strom, a NORSE HOME resident since 2003, was a founding member of Midnatsol Guild and past NORSE HOME Board Member in the 1980s. John Olsen was a Board Member (1996-2005) and his wife, Sandra, joined the NORSE HOME community in 2010. John's grandfather, Carl Knudsen, was a resident here for many years and his well-known art work is displayed on many of the walls. Carl's son, John Knudsen (John Olsen's uncle), was also a resident here until recently (1999-2011).

All who have lived at NORSE HOME seem to thrive. At one time in 2009 there were seven centenarians living at NORSE HOME. The history of NORSE HOME is a continuing modern-day saga. Although it is Norwegian in background, NORSE HOME'S roots contain the stories of all immigrant Americans.

All who work and live at the NORSE HOME will no doubt continue the longevity tradition of care and caring for each other.

OUR NORDIC HOSTS AND GUIDES

HARALD and ANNA LARRSEN and other residents, staff, Board and visitors never cease contributing to changes, growth, nurturing, and occasional surprises, all of which constitute the life of a large, welcoming facility on Seattle's scenic Phinney Ridge. And as Seattle changes, and technological and cultural waves roll in from all directions, NORSE HOME meets those challenges with professional experience, faith, a nurturing attitude, and help from the larger community.

Our hosts ANNA and HARALD almost duplicated Myrtle Varney's story (above) except for the LARSSENS' rigorous and anxious trips from Norway to America. However, the American dream encompasses everyone in time, as it has all participants in the planning and construction of NORSE HOME.

You don't need a GOLD KEY to come through the door today. Just walk in and receive a warm welcome.

JUNIUS ROCHESTER
NOVEMBER 2012

Closing Remarks

Tusen Takk!!! Mr. Junius Rochester for getting our NORSE HOME story written. This was not an easy task. It was necessary to go through many boxes of items, boxes of files, getting microfiche documents printed , and it was necessary to have the patience with our staff to attempt to choose (from hundreds) meaningful pictures to include. Congratulations, you have now become a member of the dedicated NORSE HOME enthusiasts! Many, thousand, thanks.

During the process of assisting with this project and after reading these historic pages, I believe even more in dedicating my efforts to the NORSE HOME's mission. As a matter of course in my career, I understand the need for the care and housing of our elders. The NORSE HOME ways of satisfying this need for the community was and is phenomenal. This is a result of the perseverance of its founders, the knowledge and skills of its developers, and the continual dedication of all who enter our doors. All volunteers, board members, supporting guild members, staff and residents share a passion for the NORSE HOME way of hospitality. The "we can do it" attitude by all continues to create the opportunity for serving the NORSE HOME mission and the traditions of care and caring.

We continue to update our property to be current with the senior housing community standards and still offer affordable housing. The new Flex Licensing apartments are one example. This means someone who moves into one of these apartments will no longer need to move to a different apartment when they are in need of assisted living for their ADL's (activities of daily living), as they have had to do in the recent past.

Additional thanks are necessary. Many thanks for the caring volunteer hours given by the Board of Directors past and present. They have been charged with steering the ship of caring for 55 years. It is a testament of the quality of caring from NORSE HOME staff over the years that past board members have become in the past and currently are residents.

It has been that special dedication of NORSE HOME staff that has supported the phrase "home for life." This does not just refer to the aging years of life, it refers to the quality of life at all advancing ages. There is a reason why residents thrive at NORSE HOME and a good number live past 100 years old.

So our history has been learned from old hand-written and typed letters, old dated documents, and pictorial artifacts. We are pleased to share a sample here. We look forward to the new expanded library we have planned, which will be available for persons interested in researching more information. Perhaps you will learn about your family or your friend's connections to NORSE HOME.

Please find our newest website at www.norsehome.org to see more for yourself. We have joined the social media and you can like us on Facebook to spread the word about NORSE HOME's Scandinavian hospitality to an International population.

Perhaps now you will want to reserve your own apartment, so you too can enjoy the NORSE HOME traditions of care and caring.

Gratefully yours,

JENNIFER JORGENSEN
EXECUTIVE DIRECTOR

ADDENDUM I
FIRST RESIDENTS

1957 Inaugural Residents

Andrus, Dora	6/15
Arke, Agnes M.	6/24
Backen, Martin	7/5
Baker, Courtland	7/1
Baldwin, Martha	7/9
Beall, Clifford	8/27
Berg, Ruth E.	10/16
Brammeier, Alice	8/2
Brethorst, Alice B.	6/18
Brown, Clarence	1/15
Calder, Henrietta	8/19
Chadwick, Emma	12/10
Clark, Grace M.	9/3
Crawford, Grace	12/16
Czech, Emma P.	12/2
Dahl, Louis	10/24
Dial, Mr. William H.	6/15
Dial, Mrs. William H.	6/15
Duguid, Ada C.	9/1
Dunlap, Margaret	7/1
Enge, Helen	6/17
Falk, Laura	6/17

Finnestad, Sina	6/15
Fisher, Martha L.	6/16
Foss, George G.	6/16
Fraser, William H.	11/4
Friberg, Olaf	6/24
Friberg, Ida M.	6/24
Gamlem, Marie	6/17
Garberson, Fern	9/10
Gerbing, August	6/15
Goff, Mrs. Richard	9/25
Gooding, Alice	12/5
Hadley, Pauline	12/26
Hankens, Mary A.	6/16
Harrison, Madeline	9/12
Haugen, Mrs. Toldin	7/31
Heitman, Hilda	8/31
Hemen, Martha	9/5
Hepler, Stella	8/22
Hilty, Emma	9/25
Hodges, Louise	7/1
Hoffman, Mr. Ural N.	8/2
Hoffman, Mrs. Ural N.	8/2
Honts, Ada	10/24
Hufty, Lulu	9/5
Isdahl, Magnus	7/3
Iversen, Bertha	10/8
Iversen, Edward	8/5
Jacobsen, Johanna	6/16
Johnson, Carl A.	8/7
Johnson, Mr. Lee	9/24
Johnstone, Maude E.	6/16

Keeney, Ina	6/15
Knupp, Lucy	9/ 6
Korsnes, John	6/19
Lange, Ophelia	6/16
Larsen, Albert	7/1
Larsen, Eva	7/1
Larsen, Anders	6/15
Larsen, Laura	6/22
Lattin, Beverly	7/1
Lein, Hanna	10/16
Marshall, Emily	9/21
Marshall, William	11/17
Monson, Alma L.	9/11
Morton, Dr. Warren	6/29
Morton, Mrs. Warren	6/29
Moyer, Mattie	10/31
McVeigh, Emilia	8/24
Ness, Gena	6/12
Nilsen, Mrs. O.W.	9/26
Olsen, Knut A.	9/8
Paulson, Dr. Otto	6/15
Peterson, Anna	12/6
Pontius, Pearl	6/8
Qualsund, Amanda	6/15
Ramstad, Emma G.	6/15
Randles, Mr. James	6/20
Randles, Mrs. James	6/20

Reaney, Margaret	10/1
Reedy, Josepha	10/1
Reid, Edna	8/29
Revenough, Carl	8/1
Roy, Ruth	9/30
Rutherford, Eva	7/17
Ryland, Albert S.	7/3
Scott, Charles M.	9/1
Scott, Mrs. Charles M.	9/1
Semenson, Marit	10/20
Snow, Fred J.	12/1
Sonnichsen, Sonke	9/10
Sorenson, Marie	10/21
Sorge, Louise	7/3
Stegler, Elizabeth	8/24
Sunsby, Theo N.	11/5
Sunsby, Mrs. Theo N.	11/5
Taylor, Adeline	6/15
Taylor, Tillie	6/15
Ulvestad, Mr. Karl	8/30
Ulvestad, Mrs. Karoline	8/30
Utlenweiler, Mrs. Sidonia	8/1
Vandergover, Johann	7/28
Viele, Charles	12/20
Vik, Karl J.	6/15
Vik, Mrs. Karl J.	6/15
Waltersdorph, Mrs. A.	6/21
Webster, Josephine	7/26
West, Jacob F.	8/5
Wester, Sallie	6/17
White, Zula Rae	6/15

ADDENDUM II
PRESIDENTS GALLERY

Abraham Kvalheim
1931-1940

Dr. T.W. Buschmann
1941-1954

Paul P. Berg
1955-1965

B. Thor Bjornstad
1966-1968
1970-1973

Ole J. Adreasson
1969

Albert Birkland
1974-1976

Thor Ulvstad
1977-1979

Peggy Stjern
1980-1982

Trygve Kvalheim
1983-1990
1996-1999

Trygve Jorgensen
1991-1993

Wilbur Linde
1994-1995

Bertil Lundh
1995-1996

Henry Haugen
1999-2006

Andrea Torland
2007-2010

Konrad S. Uri
2009-2013

ADDENDUM III
ADMINISTRATORS

1957 – 1959	Warren Croston
1959 – 1966	Ole Andreassen
1966 – 1973	Alberta Christensen
1973 – 1979	Arne Eilertsen
1979 – 1981	Ernest Beals
1982 – 1985	Robert Surface
1985 – 2007	Robert Solem
2008 – 2009	Interim Directors
2009 – Present	Jennifer Jorgensen

Acknowledgements

Authors encounter many challenges when researching and preparing text. But no challenge is more difficult than thanking the many individuals who make a project possible.

Please bear with me as I attempt to cite names and organizations that stand out as helpmates in looking at the past and estimating the future of NORSE HOME. Right off the top, I apologize to those few who deserve recognition, but due to my indolence or poor memory, didn't make the cut. In any case, I'm grateful beyond words for the help rendered in assembling this interesting story.

Without the support of the NORSE HOME Board of Trustees, nothing would follow this sentence. Konrad Uri, President, and his team entered this historical fray with enthusiasm, and they found funds to help build the story.

Jennifer Jorgensen, NORSE HOME Executive Director, and her Staff never balked or complained when I asked for help. Nor did they noticeably wince when I attempted to understand and record NORSE HOME activities. I had carte blanche to the building and grounds (short of invading resident privacy or professional Staff areas). Historical documents, cartons of who-knows-what, and tips on names, dates and events were consistently forthcoming. To abet my efforts, I was provided Fourth Floor storage/office space. This retreat allowed me to quickly sort material, make phone calls, and plan research excursions. Cooperative individuals on the Desk and in Maintenance, Housekeeping, the Health Center and Kitchen and Dining, buoyed my spirits.

Outside the comfortable walls of NORSE HOME, I received unstinting support from professional organizations. Many of these sources have stood by me for years when I was immersed in other projects. These groups may also have been noted in the book's SOURCES AND SELECTED BIBLIOGRAPHY, but this page will be their reliable roost. They deserve better than a cold listing by name, but with apologies, here goes:

NORSE HOME Libraries and Archives
The Seattle Public Library (several departments)
Museum of History and Industry (MOHAI) and its fine research library, Seattle
City of Seattle Municipal Archives
Washington State Archives, Puget Sound Branch
Norway Hall, Seattle
Leif Erikson Lodge No. 1, Sons of Norway, Seattle (and its cozy library)
Valkyrien Lodge No. 1, Daughters of Norway, Seattle
The Norwegian Commercial Club, Seattle
The Norwegian Male Chorus, Seattle
The Norwegian Ladies Chorus, Seattle
The Nordic Heritage Museum, Seattle (and its eclectic library, archives, and helpful staff)
Ballard Historical Society, Seattle
University of Washington Libraries (especially Special Collections Division, the Allen Library)

My colleagues in the Pacific Northwest Historians Guild, and Libraries at Pioneer Hall, home of The Pioneer Association of The State of Washington

Special Commendations are awarded by me to individuals who pleasantly sat — or stood — for interviews:

Konrad Uri, President of the Board, and Jennifer Jorgensen, NORSE HOME Executive Director, freely gave their views about our history project. They also helped select design features of the book and took responsibility for vetting and editing the draft manuscript.

Molly Holscher, Activities Director of NORSE HOME, also provided her institutional and personal memories when I needed an answer.

Claire Tadych, Public Relations Coordinator at NORSE HOME, helped me find sources and people.

Kathy Rost-Schmidt, Administrative and Marketing Assistant at NORSE HOME, was a valuable editor and organizer of final drafts and images.

Helen Buschmann Belvin, daughter of NORSE HOME founder and leader Dr. T.W. Buschmann, and her husband David and daughter Ilene Garland, allowed me to interview each of them. They also provided copies of relevant NORSE HOME letters and documents. I must add that some of those materials were copies of letters written by Helen's brother-in-law, August Buschmann, who played an important role in NORSE HOME fundraising.

John Mahlum, with his father Edward, contributed years of service to NORSE HOME. He generously turned over documents, genealogical charts and photos.

Lucille Hayes, a member of the Bjornstad family that did so much for NORSE HOME, recalled her young days as the child of Norwegian immigrants and long family walks in Woodland Park and Ballard.

Robert Allen Skotheim, former president of Whitman College, the Huntington Gallery, and Occidental College, is the son of Norwegian immigrants. Bob remembered attending Pastor Hans Stub's Immanuel Lutheran Church in Seattle. He also loaned me a book describing World War II days in Norway.

Whitman College friends Hedda and Robert R. "Pete" Reid of Walla Walla, Washington, provided the interesting details about Hedda's father, Oscar Marcos Jorgenson, who was for years "The Scandinavian Reporter" on Seattle radio stations KXA and KJR.

Inger Saltonstall, president of the Daughters of Norway of the Pacific Coast (Valkyrien Lodge No. 1) researched the Daughters' history at my request — and added other helpful information.

Trygve Kvalheim, former NORSE HOME Board member and president, provided interesting comment and photos and took a special interest in the project.

Myrtle Varney, NORSE HOME resident, remembered her youth near Woodland Park, the hamburger joint in Fremont, and the old Phinney homestead. She also shared memories of her family and friends with ties to NORSE HOME.

Lila Strom, who served many years on the NORSE HOME Board, reminisced about early years.

Anne Marie Frodesen Steiner was a special partner. She not only guided me through the maze of NORSE HOME Guilds, but edited my chapter on those important organizations, turned over copious personal files, and sent me on my way with a large slice of lemon meringue pie. I must add that Anne Marie invited me — a male interloper — to observe a meeting of the Inga Frodesen Guild at NORSE HOME.

Thomas A. Stang, my Madrona Grade School friend from Seattle's Denny-Blaine neighborhood and former Norwegian Consul, spoke to me on several occasions. He also sent me a note and commented on his father, C.A. Stang, who as Norwegian Consul, participated in several NORSE HOME events, including the freezing December 10, 1955, groundbreaking ceremony.

John Olsen, a resident of NORSE HOME and longtime Ballard loyalist, showed me his extensive photographic collection and described Norway Park and other aspects of Norwegian culture in the Pacific Northwest.

Harry Solheim came to NORSE HOME and submitted to my questions about his Norwegian roots, early celebrations and ceremonies at NORSE HOME, the Norwegian Male Chorus, the Aurora Bridge, and more.

Dr. Alf Lunder Knudsen sent me historical detail about the amazing Norwegian Male Chorus of Seattle. He also added facts about the Norwegian Ladies Chorus. Dr. Knudsen was also editor of Western Viking from 1990–1997, turning over the job to his daughter, Kathleen Knudsen. Kathleen kindly contacted me in early 2012 to clarify matters about Western Viking (which had supported NORSE HOME in stories and interviews for many years).

John Gordon Hill, film maker and former Board Chair of Cornish School, found me a copy of the 1979 Landmark Nomination Form for Norway Hall in Seattle.

Kristine Leander, author, Executive Director of the Swedish Cultural Center (Seattle), and editor of Swedish Center News, broke up her busy day to answer my questions and direct me to the Swedish Cultural Center's library.

Don Thoreson, former Board Member, responded to my questions in telephone and in personal interviews, noting why he had served on the Board (recorded in the book), among other subjects.

Cyrus Malihi, Director of Building Services, who looks after maintenance and housekeeping activities at NORSE HOME, also provided a ground-up tour of the facilities. He occasionally activated his friendly, informal courier service to help me move documents around.

Robert Solem was director of NORSE HOME for twenty-two years. By telephone from his Arizona lair (80 degrees and sunshine when we talked) he reviewed NORSE HOME stages of development during his time. His gracious, straight-forward responses were helpful.

Michael Allen and his team at the NORSE HOME front desk found answers — and individuals — whenever I asked.

Shelby Gilje and her late husband, Svein Gilje, generously left a trove of books about Norway to the NORSE HOME. I used many of them (the English language volumes) to find details and names. This might be an appropriate place to again thank the Giljes for donating their library to NORSE HOME. Svein, besides having a successful journalism career (as did Shelby), was Vice President of The Norwegian American Sesquicentennial, which celebrated 150 years of Norwegian immigration to the United States.

Among readers of the raw, early manuscript, three reliable Goats from my past offered insightful comment: Tom Kuebler, reader and writer in his own right; Richard D. Thorson, M.D., who has strong Norwegian antecedents; Johan Ekstrom, Swedish-born, who came to America more or less on the same path as other immigrants.

Without the technical wizardry and computer knowledge of Robert Hanna, I would have been under water.

Herb Krushel, Dave Friesen and their colleagues at Hignell Book Printing, Winnipeg, Canada (publisher of several of my previous books), led me by the hand, nose and ear through steps leading to publication.

Thanks to family members for their patience and tolerance during research and writing binges. My wife, Joanne, is also a competent reader/editor. As usual, she caught several nubs in the manuscript. Daughter Julie and son Steve, each with longtime Ballard credentials, frequently expressed interest in the NORSE HOME project, and joined me for lunch now and then when I emerged from sessions at NORSE HOME.

JUNIUS ROCHESTER
Seattle, Washington

Sources And Selected Bibliography

A Clearing in the Distance: Frederick Law Olmsted and America in the Nineteenth Century, Witold Rybczynski, Scribner, New York, New York, 1999

Alaska: Saga of a Bold Land, Walter R. Borneman, HarperCollins, New York, New York, 2003

Alaska-Yukon-Pacific Exposition: A Timeline History, Alan J. Stein, Paula Becker and the HistoryLink Staff, A HistoryLink Book and the University of Washington, Seattle, Washington, 2009

America-America Letters: A Norwegian-American Family Correspondence, Compiled and edited by Bjorn Gunnar Ostgard, Norwegian-American Historical Association, Northfield, Minnesota, 2001

Anna: Norse Roots in Homestead Soil, Anna Guttormsen Hought, Welcome Press, Seattle, Washington, 1986

A Social History of Scandinavian Immigration, Washington State, 1895-1910, Jorgen Dahlie, Thesis in American Studies, Washington State University, Pullman, Washington, 1967

A Time Out of Joint, J.H. Lehmann, Writer's Publishing, Seattle, Washington, 1990

The Bygdelag in America, Odd Sverre Lovoll, Norwegian-American Historical Association, by Twayne Publishers, Boston, Massachusetts, 1975

Crossing: Norwegian-American Lutheranism as a Transatlantic Tradition, Editor, Todd W. Nichol, Norwegian-American Association, Northfield, Minnesota, 2003

Early Ballard, Julie D. Pheasant-Albright, Images of America, Arcadia Publishing, Charleston, South Carolina, 2007

Family Sagas: Stories of Scandinavian Immigrants, Editor, Kristine Leander, Scandinavian Language Institute, Seattle, Washington, 1997

History of the Norwegian People in America, Olaf Morgan Norlie, Augsburg Publishing House, Minneapolis, Minnesota, 1925

History of Sons of Norway: An American Fraternal Organization of Men and Women of Norwegian Birth or Extraction, Carl G.O. Hansen, Sons of Norway Supreme Lodge, Minneapolis, Minnesota, 1944

Jewish Life and Culture in Norway: Wergeland's Legacy, Britt Ormaasen and Oskar Kvasnes, Abel Abrahamsen — Publisher, New York, New York, 2003

The Last Electric Trolley, Junius Rochester, Tommie Press, Seattle, Washington, 2002

New Land, New Lives: Scandinavian Immigrants to the Pacific Northwest, Janet E. Rasmussen, Norwegian-American Historical Association, Northfield, Minnesota, University of Washington Press, Seattle, Washington, 1997

Nordic Heritage Museum, Library, Archives and Website, Seattle, Washington, 2011

The Norseman: A Bimonthly Review, several issues, Johan Hambro, Editor, Nordmanns-Forbundet, Oslo, Norway.

Norse to the Palouse, Marvin G. Slind and Fred C. Bohm, Norlys Press, Pullman, Washington, 1990

Norway, G.B. Lampe, Editor, Grondahl and Sons Boktrykkeri, Oslo, Norway, 1945

The Norwegian-American Historical Association: 1925-1975, Odd S. Lovoll and Kenneth O. Bjork, The Norwegian-American Historical Association, Northfield, Minnesota, 1975

Norwegian-American Studies, Studies & Records, Vols. I-XXXI (especially *Vol. XXX*, 1985), Odd S. Lovoll, Editor, The Norwegian-American Historical Association, Board of Publications, Northfield, Minnesota, 1970s-1980s

Norwegian Seattle, Kristine Leander, Images of Seattle, Arcadia Publishing, Charleston, South Carolina, 2008

Ole Bull: Norway's Romantic Musician and Cosmopolitan Patriot, Einar Haugen & Camilla Cai, The University of Wisconsin Press, Madison, Wisconsin, 1993

Our Escape from Nazi-Occupied Norway, Leif Terdal, Trofford Publishing, Victoria, B.C., Canada, 2008

Pacific Fishing, Seattle, Washington, April 2011

Passport to Ballard: The Centennial Story, Kay F. Reinartz, Editor, Ballard News Tribune, Seattle, Washington, 1988

The Promise of America: A History of the Norwegian-American People, Odd S. Lovoll, University of Minnesota Press, Minneapolis, Minnesota, 1984

The Promise Fulfilled, Odd S. Lovoll, University of Minnesota, Minneapolis, Minnesota, 1998

The Prophecy: Prophecy of the Vikings — The Creation of the World, Author Unknown, Gudren, Iceland, 2001

Rogues, Buffoons & Statesmen, Gordon Newell, Superior Publishing Company, Seattle, Washington, 1975

Roots and Branches: The Religious Heritage of Washington State, David M. Buerge and Junius Rochester, Church Council of Greater Seattle, Seattle, Washington, 1988

Scandinavian Immigrants in New York, 1630-1674, John O. Evjen, Ph.D, K.C. Holter Publishing Co., Minneapolis, Minnesota, 1916 (pp. 19-139)

Scandinavian Settlements in Seattle, "Queen City of the Puget Sound," Patsy Adams Hegstad, Doctoral Dissertation, University of Washington, Seattle, Washington, 1970

Thirty Years over the Top: Scandinavian Airlines System Polar Flights, Seattle-Copenhagen, 1966-1996, Junius Rochester, SAS, Seattle, Washington, 1998

Unpublished Histories of Seattle Parks, Don Sherwood, Museum of History and Industry, Seattle, Washington, 1960s

The Vikings: The Last Pagans or the First Modern Europeans? Jonathan Clements, Carroll & Graf, Publishers, New York, New York, 2005

Washington: Images of a State's Heritage, Carlos Schwantes, Katherine Morrissey, David Nicandri, Susan Strasser, Melior Publications, Spokane, Washington, 1988

Index

Author Biography

JUNIUS ROCHESTER was born and raised in Seattle, Washington. He graduated from Seattle's Garfield High School; Whitman College, Walla Walla, Washington; and Harvard Business School, Boston, Massachusetts. He is married to Joanne Marie Elliott and is the father of three children.

Junius's paternal grandparents were Pacific Northwest pioneers. Continuing the family legacy of history and heritage, Junius holds membership in the Washington State Historical Society, the Oregon Historical Society, the Pacific Northwest Historians Guild (past president) and The Pioneer Association of the State of Washington (current president). In 1995, he was given a Project Award by the Association of King County Historical Organizations and the King County Landmarks and Heritage Commission. In 2006, Junius received an Award of Merit from the American Association for State and Local History.

After a career in international business he turned to his favorite avocations: writing and historical research. He is the author of eight books and wrote a column in the *Seattle Weekly* ("*Eminent Seattleites*"). He has also written numerous articles and over 100 historical vignettes which for seven years he read weekly on KUOW-FM, Seattle's National Public Radio outlet. Junius gives historical presentations to civic, educational and historical organizations and aboard cruise ships.

Among Junius's books: *The Last Electric Trolley, a Seattle Neighborhood History; Roots and Branches, the Religious Heritage of the Pacific Northwest; Little St. Simons Island, a History of the Georgia Sea Islands; Seattle's Best-Kept Secret, a History of The Lighthouse for the Blind, Inc.;* and *SAS, Thirty Years Over the Top, Scandinavian Airlines System Polar Flights, Seattle-Copenhagen, 1966-1996.*